Exegetical Fallacies

Exegetical Fallacies

Second Edition

D. A. Carson

Baker Books

A Division of Baker Book House Co
Grand Rapids, Michigan 49516

Published by Baker Academic
a division of Baker Book House Company
P.O. Box 6287, Grand Rapids, MI 49516-6287
www.bakeracademic.com

Seventh printing, November 2002

Printed in the United States of America

Library of Congress Cataloging-in-Publication Data

Carson, D. A.
    Exegetical fallacies / D. A. Carson.—2nd Ed.
        p.   cm.
    Includes bibliographical references.
    ISBN 0-8010-2086-7 (pbk.)
    1. Bible—Criticism, interpretation, etc. 2. Errors. I. Title.
    BS540.C36   1996
    220.6'.01—dc20   96-4156

W. Gordon Brown
In Memoriam

Contents

List of Abbreviations   *9*

Preface to the Second Edition   *11*

Preface   *13*

Introduction   *15*

1. Word-Study Fallacies   *27*
2. Grammatical Fallacies   *65*
3. Logical Fallacies   *87*
4. Presuppositional and Historical Fallacies   *125*
5. Concluding Reflections   *137*

Index of Subjects   *143*

Index of Authors   *145*

Index of Scripture   *147*

List of Abbreviations

Bauer	W. Bauer, *A Greek-English Lexicon of the New Testament*, trans. F. W. Arndt and F. W. Gingrich (1957); rev. ed., trans. F. W. Gingrich and F. W. Danker (1979)
Bib	*Biblica*
BS	*Bibliotheca Sacra*
CanJTh	*Canadian Journal of Theology*
CBQ	*Catholic Biblical Quarterly*
CT	*Christianity Today*
JBL	*Journal of Biblical Literature*
JETS	*Journal of the Evangelical Theological Society*
JTS	*Journal of Theological Studies*
LSJ	H. G. Liddell, R. Scott, H. S. Jones, *Greek-English Lexicon* (9th ed., 1940)
LXX	Septuagint
KJV	King James Version
NEB	New English Bible
NIV	New International Version
NovTest	*Novum Testamentum*
NTS	*New Testament Studies*
RestQ	*Restoration Quarterly*
SJT	*Scottish Journal of Theology*
TB	*Tyndale Bulletin*
TSF Bull	*TSF Bulletin*
WTJ	*Westminster Theological Journal*

Preface to the Second Edition

The surprising success of this book suggests that there is an encouraging number of preachers and teachers of Scripture who want to correct common errors in exegesis. I am grateful to God if this book has been a help.

Many readers have written to share with me their own lists of amusing fallacies. A few of their suggestions have found their way into the pages of this second edition. Three or four reviewers or letter writers strenuously objected to this or that example. I have tried to take their complaints to heart. In a couple of instances I have revised the section; in two or three instances I merely dropped the material or substituted better examples, not always because I thought I was wrong on the issue, but simply because in this book I am not trying to score points on particular subjects so much as give indisputable examples of exegetical fallacies. But most of the material in the first edition has been retained here. Occasionally I have dropped material not because I have changed my mind as to the exegesis, but because I would defend my position a little differently today.

By contrast, from time to time I have inserted fresh examples. In addition, the material in the fourth chapter has been expanded somewhat. Granted the rapid changes taking place in the field of hermeneutics, that chapter could easily have become a couple of books. Restraint prevailed, so that not too many pages were added.

I would have liked to expand the fifth chapter, but it seemed best not to enlarge the book too much at one go, not least because it is primarily used as auxiliary reading in exegesis courses, so that too great an increase in length would probably destroy its usefulness. In particular, I rather wanted to say more about the interpretation of literary genres than I did. The little I added may be of use to some. And if this book ever goes to a third edition, perhaps that will be the time to add more to the fifth chapter.

Soli Deo gloria

D. A. Carson

Preface

Most of the material in this book was first delivered at the Spring Lectureship sponsored by Western Conservative Baptist Seminary in Portland, Oregon, in 1983. It is a pleasure to record my thanks to James DeYoung, the chairman of the Lectureship Committee, not only for the invitation, but also for efficient arrangements and boundless courtesy. My thanks, too, to the faculty members and students who went out of their way to make me feel welcome.

Some of the material in these pages still retains elements of its genesis in lectures, although the notes, of course, played no part in the original series. Far more of my examples have been taken from New Testament scholarship than Old Testament scholarship, not only because that reflects my relative expertise, but even more because many of these examples have been drawn from classroom material culled over the years in the course of teaching students responsible exegesis of the New Testament. Although my reading of Old Testament scholarship assures me that comparable examples are no less frequent in that corpus, to prevent this book from growing out of bounds I have decided to retain the original limits.

Some of those who have heard or read part or all of this material have sometimes criticized me for being unfair to their preferred viewpoint on some theological or exegetical point. I have tried to listen to their criticisms and make changes where needed; but I am encouraged to note that approximately the same proportion of Baptists as Paedo-baptists, Calvinists as Arminians, and so forth, have voiced objections and suggestions, so perhaps the balance is not too far off. I can only insist in the strongest terms that I have tried not to use these pages as a sounding board by which to give vent to personal prejudices. Doubtless I have in some measure failed, but readers who take too great offense in discovering just where I have damaged their preferred interpretations might profitably ask themselves to what extent their own prejudices have influenced their judgment.

My secretary Marty Irwin typed the manuscript under extremely short notice and considerable pressure; I am profoundly grateful for her efficiency and enthusiasm. Mark Reasoner gave valuable assistance with two of the indexes.

Soli Deo gloria.

Introduction

To focus on fallacies, exegetical or otherwise, sounds a bit like focusing on sin: guilty parties may take grudging notice and briefly pause to examine their faults, but there is nothing intrinsically redemptive in the procedure. Nevertheless, when the sins are common and (what is more) frequently unrecognized by those who commit them, detailed description may have the salutary effect of not only encouraging thoughtful self-examination but also providing an incentive to follow a better way. I hope that by talking about what should not be done in exegesis, we may all desire more deeply to interpret the Word of God aright. If I focus on the negative, it is in the hope that readers will thereby profit more from the positive instruction they glean from texts and lectures.

Before pressing on to the study itself, I shall avoid distracting questions later if at the outset I sketch the importance of this study and the dangers inherent in it, and frankly acknowledge the many limitations I have adopted.

The Importance of This Study

This study is important because exegetical fallacies are painfully frequent among us—among us whose God-given grace and responsibility is the faithful proclamation of the Word of God. Make a mistake in the interpretation of one of Shakespeare's plays, falsely scan a piece of Spenserian verse, and there is unlikely to be an entailment of eternal consequence; but we cannot lightly accept a similar laxity in the interpretation of Scripture. We are dealing with God's thoughts: we are obligated to take the greatest pains to understand them truly and to explain them clearly. It is all the more shocking, therefore, to find in the evangelical pulpit, where the Scriptures are officially revered, frequent and inexcusable sloppiness in handling them. All of us, of course, will make some exegetical mistakes: I am painfully aware of some of my own, brought to my attention by increasing years, wider reading, and alert colleagues who love me enough to correct me. But tragic is the situation when the preacher or teacher is perpetually unaware of the blatant nonsense he utters, and of the consequent damage he inflicts on the church of God. Nor will it do to be satisfied with pointing a finger at other groups whose skills are less than our own: we must begin by cleaning up our own backyard.

The essence of all critical thought, in the best sense of that abused expression, is the justification of opinions. A critical interpretation of Scripture is one that has adequate justification—lexical, grammatical, cultural, theological, historical, geographical, or other justification.[1] In other words, critical exegesis in this sense is exegesis that provides sound reasons for the choices it makes and the positions it adopts. Critical exegesis is opposed to merely personal opinions, appeals to blind authority (the interpreter's or anyone else's), arbitrary interpretations, and speculative opinions. This is not to deny that spiritual things are spiritually discerned, or to argue that piety is irrelevant; it is to say rather that not even piety and the gift of the Holy Spirit guarantee infallible interpretations. When two equally godly interpreters emerge with mutually incompatible interpretations of a text, it must be obvious even to the most spiritual, and perhaps as well to most of those who are not devoted to the worst forms of polysemy (about which I will say a little more later), that they cannot both be right.[2] If the interpreters in ques-

---

1. For this use of the term *critical* I am relying on Bernard Ramm, *Protestant Biblical Interpretation: A Handbook of Hermeneutics for Conservative Protestants*, 2d ed. (Boston: Wilde, 1956), 101–3. This material is not found in the third edition.

2. Occasionally a remarkable blind spot prevents people from seeing this point. Almost twenty years ago I rode in a car with a fellow believer who relayed to me what the Lord had "told" him that morning in his quiet time. He had been reading the KJV of Matthew; and I perceived that not only had he misunderstood the archaic English, but also that the KJV at that place had unwittingly misrepresented the Greek text. I gently suggested there might be another way to understand the passage and summarized what I thought the passage was saying. The brother dismissed my view as impossible on the grounds that the Holy Spirit,

tion are not only spiritual but also mature, perhaps we may hope that they will probe for the reasons why they have arrived at different conclusions. With continued cautious, courteous, and honest examination, they may in time come to a resolution of the conflicting interpretative claims. Perhaps one is right and the other is wrong; perhaps both are in some measure right and wrong, and both need to change their respective positions; or perhaps the two interpreters are unable to zero in on the precise reasons why they disagree, and therefore remain unable to track down the exegetical or hermeneutical problem and resolve it. No matter: from our point of view, what is important is that the two interpreters are involved in critical exegesis, exegesis that provides, or attempts to provide, adequate justification of all conclusions reached and of every opinion held.

But if critical exegesis offers sound reasons, it must learn to reject unsound reasons. That is why this study is important. By exposing our exegetical fallacies, we may become better practitioners of critical exegesis.

Careful handling of the Bible will enable us to "hear" it a little better. It is all too easy to read the traditional interpretations we have received from others into the text of Scripture. Then we may unwittingly transfer the authority of Scripture to our traditional interpretations and invest them with a false, even an idolatrous, degree of certainty. Because traditions are reshaped as they are passed on, after a while we may drift far from God's Word while still insisting all our theological opinions are "biblical" and therefore true. If when we are in such a state we study the Bible uncritically, more than likely it will simply reinforce our errors. If the Bible is to accomplish its work of continual reformation—reformation of our lives and our doctrine—we must

---

who dies not lie, had told him the truth on this matter. Being young and bold, I pressed on with my explanation of grammar, context, and translation, but was brushed off by a reference to 1 Cor. 2:10b–15: spiritual things must be spiritually discerned—which left little doubt about my status. Genuinely intrigued, I asked this brother what he would say if I put forward my interpretation, not on the basis of grammar and text, but on the basis that the Lord himself had given me the interpretation I was advancing. He was silent a long time, and then concluded, "I guess that would mean the Spirit says the Bible means different things to different people."

do all we can to listen to it afresh and to utilize the best resources at our disposal.

The importance of this sort of study cannot be overestimated if we are to move toward unanimity on those matters of interpretation that still divide us. I speak to those with a high view of Scripture: it is very distressing to contemplate how many differences there are among us as to what Scripture actually says. The great, unifying truths should not of course be minimized; but the fact remains that among those who believe the canonical sixty-six books are nothing less than the Word of God written there is a disturbing array of mutually incompatible theological opinions. Robert K. Johnston has a point when he writes:

> [That] evangelicals, all claiming a Biblical norm, are reaching contradictory theological formulations on many of the major issues they are addressing suggests the problematic nature of their present understanding of theological interpretation. To argue that the Bible is authoritative, but to be unable to come to anything like agreement on what it says (even with those who share an evangelical commitment), is self-defeating.[3]

This may not be very carefully worded: the self-defeat to which Johnston refers may be hermeneutical and exegetical; it has no necessary bearing on the Bible's authority. But he does help us face up to some embarrassing disarray.

Why is it that among those with equally high views of Scripture's authority there are people who think tongues are the definitive sign of the baptism of the Spirit, others who think the gift of tongues is optional, and still others who think it no longer exists as a genuine gift? Why are there some who hold to a dispensational approach to Scripture, and others who call themselves covenant theologians? Why are there several brands of Calvinists and Arminians, Baptists and Paedo-baptists? Why do some stoutly defend a Presbyterian form of church government, others press for some form of congregationalism, and still others defend the three offices and hierarchical structure that dominated the West for almost a millennium and a half from the time of the subapostolic fathers on? Dare I ask what is the sig-

3. Robert K. Johnston, *Evangelicals at an Impasse: Biblical Authority in Practice* (Atlanta: John Knox, 1979), vii–viii.

nificance of the Lord's Supper? Or why there is such a plethora of opinions regarding eschatology?

In one sense, of course, the reasons are not always rational, or amenable to correction by improved exegetical rigor alone. Many local Bible teachers and preachers have never been forced to confront alternative interpretations at full strength; and because they would lose a certain psychological security if they permitted their own questions, aroused by their own reading of Scripture, to come into full play, they are unlikely to throw over received traditions. But I am not talking about such people. I am restricting myself for the sake of this discussion to the wisest, most mature, best trained, and most devout leaders of each position: why cannot they move to greater unanimity on all kinds of doctrinal fronts?

Superficially, of course, there may be several purely practical hurdles to overcome. The leaders may not feel they have the time to spend in the kind of quality discussion that could win breakthroughs. Probably most of them think the other person is so set in his or her ways that there is little to be gained by attempting such a dialogue—all the while feeling quite certain that most if not all the movement should come from the opponents, who ought to admit to the errors of their ways and adopt the true position! Others might feel too insecure in their position to venture into debate. But if we could remove all of those kinds of hindrances, the most crucial causes of doctrinal division among these hypothetical leaders who have now (in our imagination) gathered for humble, searching discussions in an effort to heal their divisions would be differences of opinion as to what this passage or that passage actually says, or as to how this passage and that passage relate to each other.

It is possible, of course, that frank, extended debate might at first do no more than expose the nature of the differences, or how interwoven they are with broader questions. Ultimately, however, once all those tributaries have been carefully and humbly explored, each raising difficult exegetical questions of its own, the remaining debates among those who hold a high view of Scripture will be exegetical and hermeneutical, nothing else. Even if our theoretical opponents succeed only in getting to the place where they decide the exegetical evidence is insufficient to reach a sure decision, they will have gained something;

for that position, honestly held on both sides, would mean that neither party has the right, on biblical grounds, to exclude the other.

From time to time I have been involved in such talks; indeed, occasionally I have sought them out. Sometimes it is impossible to get very far: the emotional hurdles are too high, or the potential time commitment to win unanimity too great. But where immensely profitable conversations have taken place, there has always been on both sides a growing ability to distinguish a good argument from a bad one, a strong argument from a weak one. It follows, then, that the study of exegetical fallacies is important. Perhaps we shall find extra incentive in this study if we recall how often Paul exhorts the Philippian believers to be like-minded, to think the same thing—an exhortation that goes beyond mere encouragement to be mutually forbearing, but one that demands that we learn to move toward unanimity in the crucial business of thinking God's thoughts after him. This, surely, is part of the discipline of loving God with our minds.

Like much of our theology, our exegetical practices in most cases have been passed on to us by teachers who learned them many years earlier. Unless both our teachers and we ourselves have kept up, it is all too likely that our exegetical skills have not been honed by recent developments. Hermeneutics, linguistics, literary studies, greater grammatical sophistication, and advances in computer technology have joined forces to demand that we engage in self-criticism of our exegetical practices. Moreover, some of the developments have so spilled over into broader areas of Christian endeavor (e.g., the impact of the new hermeneutic on our understanding of contextualization in world missions) that mature thought is urgently required. The sum total of all useful exegetical knowledge did not reach its apex during the Reformation, nor even in the past century. As much as we can and must learn from our theological forebears, we face the harsh realities of this century; and neither nostalgia nor the preferred position of an ostrich will remove either the threats or the opportunities that summon our exegetical skills to new rigor.

These last two considerations remind me of the observation of David Hackett Fischer, who addresses himself rather acidly to his fellow historians:

Historians must, moreover, develop critical tests not merely for their interpretations, but also for their methods of arriving at them. . . . Among my colleagues, it is common to believe that any procedure is permissible, as long as its practitioner publishes an essay from time to time, and is not convicted of a felony. The resultant condition of modern historiography is that of the Jews under the Judges: every man does that which is right in his own eyes. The fields are sown with salt, and plowed with the heifer, and there is a famine upon the land.[4]

I am unprepared to say whether the plight of exegesis is more or less secure than that of historiography; but certainly there are painful similarities.

The final reason why this study has become important is the change in theological climate in the Western world during the past thirty or forty years. At the risk of oversimplification, one could argue that the generation of conservative Christians before the present one faced opponents who argued in effect that the Bible is not trustworthy, and only the ignorant and the blind could claim it is. In the present generation, there are of course many voices that say the same thing; but there are new voices that loudly insist our real problem is hermeneutical and exegetical. Conservatives, we are told, have not properly understood the Bible. They have imposed on the sacred text an artificial notion of authority and a forced exegesis of passage after passage. One of the emphases of the acerbic attack on "fundamentalism" by James Barr is that conservatives do not really understand the Bible, that they use critical tools inconsistently and even dishonestly.[5] At another level, one of the explicit claims of the recent commentary on Matthew by Robert H. Gundry is that his approach to the text is more faithful to Scripture than that of traditional conservative commentators.[6] Similar phenomena are legion.

What this means is that a traditional apologetic in such cases is irrelevant. We have been outflanked on the hermeneutical and exegetical fronts, and one of the steps we must take to get

4. David Hackett Fischer, *Historians' Fallacies: Toward a Logic of Historical Thought* (New York: Harper and Row, 1970), xix–xx.
5. James Barr, *Fundamentalism* (London: SCM, 1977).
6. Robert H. Gundry, *Matthew: A Commentary on His Literary and Theological Art* (Grand Rapids: Eerdmans, 1982).

back into the discussion is to examine our own exegetical and hermeneutical tools afresh. This includes the rigorous exposure of bad or weak arguments, whether our own or those of others.

The Dangers of This Study

If there are reasons why a study of exegetical fallacies is important, there are also reasons why such a study is dangerous.

The first is that persistent negativism is spiritually perilous. The person who makes it his life's ambition to discover all the things that are wrong—whether wrong with life or wrong with some part of it, such as exegesis—is exposing himself to spiritual destruction. Thankfulness to God both for good things and for his sovereign protection and purpose even in bad things will be the first virtue to go. It will be quickly followed by humility, as the critic, deeply knowledgeable about faults and fallacies (especially those of others!), comes to feel superior to those whom he criticizes. Spiritual one-upmanship is not a Christian virtue. Sustained negativism is highly calorific nourishment for pride. I have not observed that seminary students, not to say seminary lecturers, are particularly exempt from this danger.

On the other hand, extended concentration on errors and fallacies may produce quite a different effect in some people. In those who are already unsure of themselves or deeply in awe of the responsibilities that weigh on the shoulders of those commissioned to preach the whole counsel of God, a study like this may drive them to discouragement, even despair. The sensitive student may ask, "If there are so many exegetical traps, so many hermeneutical pitfalls, how can I ever be confident that I am rightly interpreting and preaching the Scriptures? How can I avoid the dreadful burden of teaching untruth, of laying on the consciences of Christ's people things Christ does not himself impose, or removing what he insists should be borne? How much damage might I do by my ignorance and exegetical clumsiness?"

To such students, I can only say that you will make more mistakes if you fail to embark on such a study as this than you will if you face the tough questions and improve your skills. The big difference is that in the former case you will not be aware of the mistakes you are making. If you are genuinely concerned about the quality of your ministry, and not just about your own psychological insecurity, that will be an unacceptable alternative. Ignorance may be bliss, but it is not a virtue.

The fundamental danger with all critical study of the Bible lies in what hermeneutical experts call distanciation. Distanciation is a necessary component of critical work; but it is difficult and sometimes costly.

We gain a glimpse of what is at stake when we consider a common phenomenon at Christian seminaries.

Ernest Christian was converted as a high school senior. He went to college and studied computer science; but he also worked hard at his church and enjoyed effective ministry in the local Inter-Varsity group. His prayer times were warm and frequent. Despite occasional dearth, he often felt when he read his Bible as if the Lord were speaking to him directly. Still, there was so much of the Bible that he did not understand. As he began to reach the settled conviction that he should pursue full-time Christian ministry, his local congregation confirmed him in his sense of gifts and calling. Deeply aware of his limitations, he headed off to seminary with all the eagerness of a new recruit.

After Ernest has been six months at seminary, the picture is very different. Ernest is spending many hours a day memorizing Greek morphology and learning the details of the itinerary of Paul's second missionary journey. Ernest has also begun to write exegetical papers; but by the time he has finished his lexical study, his syntactical diagram, his survey of critical opinions, and his evaluation of conflicting evidence, somehow the Bible does not feel as alive to him as it once did. Ernest is troubled by this; he finds it more difficult to pray and witness than he did before he came to seminary. He is not sure why this is so: he does not sense the fault to be in the lecturers, most of whom seem to be godly, knowledgeable, and mature believers.

More time elapses. Ernest Christian may do one of several things. He may retreat into a defensive pietism that boisterously denounces the arid intellectualism he sees all around him; or he may be sucked into the vortex of a kind of intellectual commitment that squeezes out worship, prayer, witness, and meditative reading of Scripture; or he may stagger along until he is rescued by graduation and returns to the real world. But is there a better way? And are such experiences a necessary component of seminary life?

The answer is yes on both scores. Such experiences are necessary: they are caused by distanciation. Yet understanding the process can enable us to handle it better than would otherwise be the case. Whenever we try to understand the thought of a text (or of another person, for that matter), if we are to understand it critically—that is, not in some arbitrary fashion, but with sound reasons, and as the author meant it in the first place—we must first of all grasp the nature and degree of the differences that separate our understanding from the understanding of the text. Only then can we profitably fuse our horizon of understanding with the horizon of understanding of the text—that is, only then can we begin to shape our thoughts by the thoughts of the text so that we truly understand them. Failure to go through the distanciation before the fusion usually means there has been no real fusion: the interpreter thinks he knows what the text means, but all too often he or she has simply imposed his own thoughts onto the text.

It follows that if an institution is teaching you to think critically (as I have used that term), you will necessarily face some dislocation and disturbing distanciation. A lesser institution may not be quite so upsetting: students are simply encouraged to learn, but not to evaluate.

Distanciation is difficult, and can be costly. But I cannot too strongly emphasize that it is not an end in itself. Its proper correlative is the fusion of horizons of understanding. Provided that part of the task of interpretation is nurtured along with distanciation, distanciation will not prove destructive. Indeed, the Christian life, faith, and thought that emerge from this double-barreled process will be more robust, more spiritually alert, more discerning, more biblical, and more critical than it could otherwise have been. But some of the steps along the way are dangerous: work hard at integrating your entire Christian walk and commitment, and the topic of this study will prove beneficial. Fail to work hard at such integration and you invite spiritual shipwreck.

The Limits of This Study

This is not a highly technical discussion. It is designed for seminary students and others who take seriously their responsibility to interpret the Scriptures; but it adds nothing to the knowledge of experts.

Perhaps I should add that the title, *Exegetical Fallacies* (not *Hermeneutical Fallacies*), focuses on the practitioner. At the risk of making an oversimplified disjunction, I state that exegesis is concerned with actually interpreting the text, whereas hermeneutics is concerned with the nature of the interpretative process. Exegesis concludes by saying, "This passage means such and such"; hermeneutics ends by saying, "This interpretative process is constituted by the following techniques and pre-understandings." The two are obviously related. But although hermeneutics is an important discipline in its own right, ideally it is never an end in itself: it serves exegesis. In one sense, since I am discussing various aspects of the interpretative process, this is a hermeneutical study; however, since my focus here is not the interpretative process theoretically considered, but the practitioner who must explain what the sacred text means, I have slanted the presentation to the exegetical side of the spectrum.

Because this is not a technical study, I have not provided extensive bibliographical information. I have included only those works actually cited or referred to (however obliquely) in the presentation.

This study focuses on exegetical fallacies, not on historical and theological fallacies, except insofar as the latter impinge on the former.

I make no claim to comprehensiveness in the kind of error discussed in this book. Entries are treated because in my experience they are among the most common.

However, I have tried to be evenhanded in my examples. I have cited exegetical fallacies drawn from the works of liberals and of conservatives, the writings of Calvinists and of Arminians. Relatively unknown persons are mentioned, and so are world-class scholars. Two of my own exegetical errors receive dishonorable burial. By and large my examples have been drawn from fairly serious sources, not popular publications where the frequency of error is much higher; but I have also included a few examples from popular preachers. A slight majority of examples come from evangelical writers, but that reflects the audience for which the material was first prepared.

There is no sustained discussion in these pages of the Holy Spirit's role in our exegetical task. That subject is important and difficult, but it involves a shift to a hermeneutical focus that would detract from the usefulness of this book as a practitioner's manual.

In short, this is an amateur's collection of exegetical fallacies.

1

Word-Study Fallacies

What amazing things words are! They can convey information and express or elicit emotion. They are the vehicles that enable us to think. With words of command we can cause things to be accomplished; with words of adoration we praise God; and in another context the same words blaspheme him.

Words are among the preacher's primary tools—both the words he studies and the words with which he explains his studies. Mercifully, there now exist several excellent volumes to introduce the student to the general field of lexical semantics and to warn against particular abuses;[1] and this is all to the good, for Nathan Söderblom was right when he said, "Philology is the eye of the needle through which every theological camel must enter the heaven of theology."[2]

1. See especially the works to which repeated reference will be made: James Barr, *The Semantics of Biblical Language* (Oxford: Oxford University Press, 1961); Eugene A. Nida and Charles R. Taber, *The Theology and Practice of Translation* (Leiden: Brill, 1974); Stephen Ullmann, *Semantics: An Introduction to the Science of Meaning* (Oxford: Blackwell, 1972); G. B. Caird, *The Language and Imagery of the Bible* (London: Duckworth, 1980); Arthur Gibson, *Biblical Semantic Logic: A Preliminary Analysis* (New York: St. Martin, 1981); J. P. Louw, *Semantics of New Testament Greek* (Philadelphia: Fortress; Chico, Calif.: Scholars Press, 1982); and especially Moisés Silva, *Biblical Words and Their Meaning: An Introduction to Lexical Semantics* (Grand Rapids: Zondervan, 1983).

2. "Die Philologie ist das Nadelöhr, durch das jedes theologische Kamel in den Himmel der Gottesgelehrheit eingehen muss." Cited by J. M. van Veen, *Nathan Söderblom* (Amsterdam: H. J. Paris, 1940), 59 n. 4; cited also by A. J. Malherbe, "Through the Eye of the Needle: Simplicity or Singleness," *RestQ* 56 (1971): 119.

My own pretensions are modest. I propose merely to list and describe a collection of common fallacies that repeatedly crop up when preachers and others attempt word studies of biblical terms, and to provide some examples. The entries may serve as useful warning flags.

Common Fallacies in Semantics

1. The root fallacy

One of the most enduring of errors, the root fallacy presupposes that every word actually *has* a meaning bound up with its shape or its components. In this view, meaning is determined by etymology; that is, by the root or roots of a word. How many times have we been told that because the verbal cognate of ἀπόστολος (*apostolos*, apostle) is ἀποστέλλω (*apostellō*, I send), the root meaning of "apostle" is "one who is sent"? In the preface of the *New King James Bible*, we are told that the "literal" meaning of μονογενής (*monogenēs*) is "only begotten."[3] Is that true? How often do preachers refer to the verb ἀγαπάω (*agapaō*, to love), contrast it with φιλέω (*phileō*, to love), and deduce that the text is saying something about a special kind of loving, for no other reason than that ἀγαπάω (*agapaō*) is used?

All of this is linguistic nonsense. We might have guessed as much if we were more acquainted with the etymology of English words. Anthony C. Thiselton offers by way of example our word *nice*, which comes from the Latin *nescius*, meaning "ignorant."[4] Our "good-bye" is a contraction for Anglo-Saxon "God be with you." Now it may be possible to trace out diachronically just how *nescius* generated "nice"; it is certainly easy to imagine how "God be with you" came to be contracted to "good-bye." But I know of no one today who in saying such and such a person is "nice" believes that he or she has in some measure labeled that person ignorant because the "root meaning" or "hidden meaning" or "literal meaning" of "nice" is "ignorant."

3. *The New King James Bible* (Nashville: Nelson, 1982) or the *Revised Authorized Version* (London: Bagster, 1982), iv.
4. Anthony C. Thiselton, "Semantics and New Testament Interpretation," in *New Testament Interpretation: Essays on Principles and Methods*, ed. I. Howard Marshall (Exeter: Paternoster; Grand Rapids: Eerdmans, 1977), 80–81.

J. P. Louw provides a fascinating example.[5] In 1 Corinthians 4:1 Paul writes of himself, Cephas, Apollos, and other leaders in these terms: "So then, men ought to regard us as servants (ὑπηρέτας, *hypēretas*) of Christ and as those entrusted with the secret things of God" (NIV). More than a century ago, R. C. Trench popularized the view that ὑπηρέτης (*hypēretēs*) derives from the verb ἐρέσσω (*eressō*) "to row."[6] The basic meaning of ὑπηρέτης (*hypēretēs*), then, is "rower." Trench quite explicitly says a ὑπηρέτης (*hypēretēs*) "was originally the rower (from ἐρέσσω [*eressō*])." A. T. Robertson and J. B Hofmann went further and said ὑπηρέτης (*hypēretēs*) derives morphologically from ὑπό (*hypo*) and ἐρέτης (*eretēs*).[7] Now ἐρέσσω (*eressō*) means "rower" in Homer (eighth century B.C.!); and Hofmann draws the explicit connection with the morphology, concluding a ὑπηρέτης (*hypēretēs*) was basically an "under rower" or "assistant rower" or "subordinate rower." Trench had not gone so far: he did not detect in ὑπό (*hypo*) any notion of subordination. Nevertheless Leon Morris concluded that a ὑπηρέτης (*hypēretēs*) was "a servant of a lowly kind";[8] and William Barclay plunged further and designated ὑπηρέτης (*hypēretēs*) as "a rower on the lower bank of a trireme."[9] Yet the fact remains that with only one possible exception—and it is merely possible, not certain[10]—ὑπηρέτης (*hypēretēs*) is never used for "rower" in classical literature, and it is certainly not used that way in the New Testament. The ὑπηρέτης (*hypēretēs*) in the New Testament is a servant, and often there is little if anything to distinguish him from a διάκονος (*diakonos*). As Louw remarks, to derive the meaning of ὑπηρέτης (*hypēretēs*) from ὑπό (*hypo*) and ἐρέτης

---

5. Louw, *Semantics of New Testament Greek*, 26–27.

6. R. C. Trench, *Synonyms of the New Testament* (1854; Marshalltown: NFCE, n.d.), 32.

7. A. T. Robertson, *Word Pictures in the New Testament*, 4 vols. (Nashville: Broadman, 1931), 4:102; J. B. Hofmann, *Etymologisches Wörterbuch des Griechischen* (Munich: Oldenbourg, 1950), s.v.

8. Leon Morris, *The First Epistle of Paul to the Corinthians*, Tyndale New Testament Commentary series (Grand Rapids: Eerdmans, 1958), 74.

9. William Barclay, *New Testament Words* (Philadelphia: Westminister, 1975), s.v.

10. The inscription in question reads τοὶ ὑπηρέται τᾶν μακρᾶν ναῶν (*toi hypēretai tan makran naōn*, "the attendants [rowers?] on the large vessels"). According to LSJ, 1872, the meaning *rowers* is dubious.

(*eretēs*) is no more intrinsically realistic than deriving the meaning of "butterfly" from "butter" and "fly," or the meaning of "pineapple" from "pine" and "apple."[11] Even those of us who have never been to Hawaii recognize that pineapples are not a special kind of apple that grows on pines.

The search for hidden meanings bound up with etymologies becomes even more ludicrous when two words with entirely different meanings share the same etymology. James Barr draws attention to the pair לֶחֶם (*leḥem*) and מִלְחָמָה (*milḥāmâ*), which mean "bread" and "war" respectively:

> It must be regarded as doubtful whether the influence of their common root is of any importance semantically in classical Hebrew in the normal usage of the words. And it would be utterly fanciful to connect the two as mutually suggestive or evocative, as if battles were normally for the sake of bread or bread a necessary provision for battles. Words containing similar sound sequences may of course be deliberately juxtaposed for assonance, but this is a special case and separately recognizable.[12]

Perhaps I should return for a moment to my first three examples. It is arguable that although ἀπόστολος (*apostolos*, apostle) is cognate with ἀποστέλλω (*apostellō*, I send), New Testament use of the noun does not center on the meaning *the one sent* but on "messenger." Now a messenger is usually sent; but the word *messenger* also calls to mind the message the person carries, and suggests he represents the one who sent him. In other words, actual usage in the New Testament suggests that ἀπόστολος (*apostolos*) commonly bears the meaning a *special representative* or a *special messenger* rather than "someone sent out."

The word μονογενής (*monogenēs*) is often thought to spring from μόνος (*monos*, only) plus γεννάω (*gennaō*, to beget); and hence its meaning is "only begotten." Even at the etymological level, the γεν (*gen*)-root is tricky: μονογενής (*monogenēs*) could as easily spring from μόνος (*monos*, only) plus γένος (*genos*, kind or race) to mean "only one of its kind," "unique," or the like. If we press on to consider usage, we discover that the Septuagint renders יָחִיד (*yāḥîd*) as "alone" or "only" (e.g., Ps. 22:20 [21:21,

11. Louw, *Semantics of New Testament Greek*, 27.
12. Barr, *The Semantics of Biblical Language*, 102.

LXX, "my precious life" (NIV) or "my only soul"]; Ps. 25:16 [24:16, LXX, "for I am lonely and poor"]), without even a hint of "begetting." True, in the New Testament the word often refers to the relationship of child to parent; but even here, care must be taken. In Hebrews 11:17 Isaac is said to be Abraham's μονογενής (*monogenēs*)—which clearly cannot mean "only-begotten son," since Abraham also sired Ishmael and a fresh packet of progeny by Keturah (Gen. 25:1–2). Issac is, however, Abraham's *unique* son, his special and well-beloved son.[13] The long and short of the matter is that renderings such as "for God so loved the world that he gave his one and only Son" (John 3:16, NIV) are prompted by neither an inordinate love of paraphrase, nor a perverse desire to deny some cardinal truth, but by linguistics.

In a similar vein, although it is doubtless true that the entire range of ἀγαπάω (*agapaō*, to love) and the entire range of φιλέω (*phileō*, to love) are not exactly the same, nevertheless they enjoy substantial overlap; and where they overlap, appeal to a "root meaning" in order to discern a difference is fallacious. In 2 Samuel 13 (LXX), both ἀγαπάω (*agapaō*, to love) and the cognate ἀγάπη (*agapē*, love) can refer to Amnon's incestuous rape of his half sister Tamar (2 Sam. 13:15, LXX). When we read that

13. For further discussion, see Dale Moody, "The Translation of John 3:16 in the Revised Standard Version," *JBL* 72 (1953): 213–19. Attempts to overturn Moody's work have not been convincing. The most recent of these is by John V. Dahms, "The Johannine Use of *Monogenēs* Reconsidered," *NTS* 29 (1983): 222–32. This is not the place to enter into a point-by-point refutation of his article; but in my judgment his weighing of the evidence is not always even-handed. For instance, when he comments on the use of μονογενής *(monogenēs)* in Ps. 22:20, he stresses that things, not persons, are in view; yet when he comes to Ps. 25:16 (24:16, LXX) — "Look upon me and have mercy upon me for I am μονογενής [*monogenēs*] and poor" —he concedes the meaning *lonely* is possible but adds: "We think it not impossible that the meaning 'only child', i.e. one who has no sibling to provide help, is (also?) intended" (p. 224). Dahms argues this despite the fact that David wrote the psalm, and David had many siblings. But at least Dahms recognizes that "meaning is determined by usage, not etymology" (p. 223); and that is my main point here. Moody argues that it was the Arian controversy that prompted translators (in particular Jerome) to render μονογενής *(monogenēs)* by *unigenitus* (only begotten), not *unicus* (only); and even here, Jerome was inconsistent, for he still preferred the latter in passages like Luke 7:12; 8:42; 9:38, where the reference is not to Christ, and therefore no christological issue is involved. This rather forcefully suggests that it was not linguistic study that prompted Jerome's changes, but the pressure of contemporary theological debate.

Demas forsook Paul because he loved this present, evil world, there is no linguistic reason to be surprised that the verb is ἀγα- πάω (*agapaō*, 2 Tim. 4:10). John 3:35 records that the Father loves the Son and uses the verb ἀγαπάω (*agapaō*); John 5:20 repeats the thought, but uses φιλέω (*phileō*)—without any discernible shift in meaning. The false assumptions surrounding this pair of words are ubiquitous; and so I shall return to them again. My only point here is that there is nothing intrinsic to the verb ἀγαπάω (*agapaō*) or the noun ἀγάπη (*agapē*) to prove its real meaning or hidden meaning refers to some special kind of love.

I hasten to add three caveats to this discussion. First, I am not saying that any word can mean anything. Normally we observe that any individual word has a certain limited semantic range, and the context may therefore modify or shape the meaning of a word only within certain boundaries. The total semantic range is not permanently fixed, of course; with time and novel usage, it may shift considerably. Even so, I am not suggesting that words are infinitely plastic. I am simply saying that the meaning of a word cannot be reliably determined by etymology, or that a root, once discovered, always projects a certain semantic load onto any word that incorporates that root. Linguistically, meaning is not an intrinsic possession of a word; rather, "it is a set of relations for which a verbal symbol is a sign."[14] In one sense, of course, it is legitimate to say "this word means such and such," where we are either providing the lexical range inductively observed or specifying the meaning of a word in a particular context; but we must not freight such talk with too much etymological baggage.

The second caveat is that the meaning of a word *may* reflect the meanings of its component parts. For example, the verb ἐκ- βάλλω (*ekballō*), from ἐκ (*ek*) and βάλλω (*ballō*), does in fact mean "I cast out," "I throw out," or "I put out." The meaning of a word *may* reflect its etymology; and it must be admitted that this is more common in synthetic languages like Greek or German, with their relatively high percentages of transparent words (words that have some kind of natural relation to their meaning) than in a language like English, where words are opaque (i.e.,

14. Eugene A. Nida, *Exploring Semantic Structures* (Munich: Fink, 1975), 14.

without any natural relation to their meaning).[15] Even so, my point is that we cannot responsibly *assume* that etymology is related to meaning. We can only test the point by discovering the meaning of a word inductively.

Finally, I am far from suggesting that etymological study is useless. It is important, for instance, in the diachronic study of words (the study of words as they occur across long periods of time), in the attempt to specify the earliest attested meaning, in the study of cognate languages, and especially in attempts to understand the meanings of *hapax legomena* (words that appear only once). In the last case, although etymology is a clumsy tool for discerning meaning, the lack of comparative material means we sometimes have no other choice. That is why, as Moisés Silva points out in his excellent discussion of these matters, etymology plays a much more important role in the determination of meaning in the Hebrew Old Testament than in the Greek New Testament: the Hebrew contains proportionately far more *hapax legomena*.[16] "The relative value of this use of etymology varies inversely with the quantity of material available for the language."[17] And in any case, specification of the meaning of a word on the sole basis of etymology can never be more than an educated guess.

2. Semantic anachronism

This fallacy occurs when a late use of a word is read back into earlier literature. At the simplest level, it occurs within the same language, as when the Greek early church fathers use a word in a manner not demonstrably envisaged by the New Testament writers. It is not obvious, for instance, that their use of ἐπίσκοπος (*episkopos*, bishop) to designate a church leader who has oversight over several local churches has any New Testament warrant.

But the problem has a second face when we also add a change of language. Our word *dynamite* is etymologically derived from δύναμις (*dynamis*, power, or even miracle). I do not know how many times I have heard preachers offer some

---

15. See especially the discussion in Ullmann, *Semantics*, 80–115.
16. Silva, *Biblical Words and Their Meaning*, 38–51.
17. Ibid., 42.

such rendering of Romans 1:16 as this: "I am not ashamed of the gospel, for it is the *dynamite* of God unto salvation for everyone who believes"—often with a knowing tilt of the head, as if something profound or even esoteric has been uttered. This is not just the old root fallacy revisited. It is worse: it is an appeal to a kind of reverse etymology, the root fallacy compounded by anachronism. Did Paul think of dynamite when he penned this word? And in any case, even to mention dynamite as a kind of analogy is singularly inappropriate. Dynamite blows things up, tears things down, rips out rock, gouges holes, destroys things. The power of God concerning which Paul speaks he often identifies with the power that raised Jesus from the dead (e.g., Eph. 1:18–20); and as it operates in us, its goal is εἰς σωτηρίαν (*eis sōtē-rian*,"unto salvation," Rom. 1:16, KJV), aiming for the wholeness and perfection implicit in the consummation of our salvation. Quite apart from the semantic anachronism, therefore, dynamite appears inadequate as a means of raising Jesus from the dead or as a means of conforming us to the likeness of Christ. Of course, what preachers are trying to do when they talk about dynamite is give some indication of the greatness of the power involved. Even so, Paul's measure is not dynamite, but the empty tomb. In exactly the same way, it is sheer semantic anachronism to note that in the text "God loves a cheerful giver" (2 Cor. 9:7) the Greek word behind "cheerful" is ἱλαρόν (*hilaron*) and conclude that what God really loves is a hilarious giver. Perhaps we should play a laugh-track record while the offering plate is being circulated.

A third level of the same problem was painfully exemplified in three articles about blood in *Christianity Today*.[18] The authors did an admirable job of explaining the wonderful things science has discovered that blood can do—in particular its cleansing role as it flushes out cellular impurities and transports nourishment to every part of the body. What a wonderful picture (we were told) of how the blood of Jesus Christ purifies us from every sin (1 John 1:7). In fact, it is nothing of the kind. Worse, it is irresponsibly mystical and theologically misleading. The

---

18. Paul Brand and Philip Yancey, "Blood: The Miracle of Cleansing," *CT* 27/4 (Feb. 18, 1983): 12–15; "Blood: The Miracle of Life," *CT* 27/5 (Mar. 4, 1983): 38–42; "Life in the Blood," *CT* 27/6 (Mar. 18, 1983): 18–21.

phrase the *blood of Jesus* refers to Jesus' violent, sacrificial death.[19] In general, the blessings that the Scriptures show to be accomplished or achieved by the blood of Jesus are equally said to be accomplished or achieved by the death of Jesus (e.g., justification, Rom. 3:21–26; 5:6–9; redemption, Rom. 3:24; Eph. 1:7; Rev. 5:9). If John tells us that the blood of the Lord Jesus Christ purifies us from every sin, he is informing us that our hope for continued cleansing and forgiveness rests not on protestations of our goodness while our life is a sham (1 John 1:6, probably directed against proto-Gnostics) but on continual walking in the light and on continued reliance on Christ's finished work on the cross.

3. Semantic obsolescence

In some ways, this fallacy is the mirror image of semantic anachronism. Here the interpreter assigns to a word in his text a meaning that the word in question used to have in earlier times, but that is no longer found within the live, semantic range of the word. That meaning, in other words, is semantically obsolete.

One of the more interesting lexical works on my shelves is a *Dictionary of Obsolete English*.[20] Some words, of course, simply lose their usefulness and drop out of the language (e.g., "to chaffer," meaning to "to bargain, haggle, dispute"); far trickier are those that remain in the language but change their meaning.[21] So also in the biblical languages: Homeric words no longer found in the Septuagint or the New Testament are of relatively little interest to the biblical specialist, but a Hebrew word that means one thing at an early stage of the written language and another at a later stage, or a Greek word that means one thing in classical Greek and another in the New Testament, can easily lead the unwary into the pitfall of this third fallacy.

19. See Alan Stibbs, *The Meaning of the Word 'Blood' in the Scripture* (London: Tyndale, 1954).

20. R. C. Trench, *Dictionary of Obsolete English* (reprint; New York: Philosophical Library, 1958).

21. For example, "nephew" could at one time refer to a grandson or an even more remote lineal descendant; "pomp" at one time meant "procession" without any overtones of garish display. For excellent discussion on the problem of change of meaning in words, refer to Ullmann, *Semantics*, 193–235.

Some changes are fairly easy to plot. The Greek μάρτυς (*martys*) stands behind our English word *martyr*. The plot of the development of the Greek noun and its cognate verb has often been traced[22] and runs something like this:

a. one who gives evidence, in or out of court
b. one who gives solemn witness or affirmation (e.g., of one's faith)
c. one who witnesses to personal faith, even in the threat of death
d. one who witnesses to personal faith by the acceptance of death
e. one who dies for a cause—a "martyr"

This development was certainly not smooth. At a given period, one person might use μάρτυς (*martys*) one way, and another person use it some other way; or the same person might use the word in more than one way, depending on the context. In this case, development was doubtless retarded by the fact that the witness of stage c was often before a court of law, reminiscent of state a. Certainly by the time that the *Martyrdom of Polycarp* 1:1; 19:1 (mid-second century) was written, the final stage had been reached. The standard classical Greek lexicon urges that stage e was reached by the time the Book of Revelation was penned: the church at Pergamum did not renounce its faith in Christ, "even in the days of Antipas, my faithful μάρτυς [*martys*, witness? martyr?], who was put to death in your city" (2:13). The conclusion may be premature: in the passage about the two witnesses, they *complete* their witness *before* they are killed (11:7), which suggests a place on the plot no more advanced than stage c. Perhaps, therefore, the word μάρτυς (*martys*) in Revelation 2:13 should simply be rendered "witness"; or perhaps in John's usage the term has a semantic range that includes several different stages.[23]

In short, words change their meaning over time. Most of us are aware by now that the force of diminutive suffixes had

22. Caird, *Language and Imagery*, 65–66. See also Alison A. Trites, *The New Testament Concept of Witness* (Cambridge: University Press, 1977).
23. The English word *martyr* has gone to a further stage, stage f if you will, found in snappish expressions such as "Oh, stop being a martyr!" which means, roughly, "Stop feeling sorry for yourself."

36

largely dissipated by the time the New Testament was written: it is difficult to distinguish ὁ παῖς (*ho pais*) from τὸ παιδίον (*to paidion*) by age or size. We are also aware that many perfective prefixes had lost some or all of their force.

It follows, then, that we should be a trifle suspicious when any piece of exegesis tries to establish the meaning of a word by appealing first of all to its usage in classical Greek rather than to its usage in Hellenistic Greek. In an article in *Christianity Today*, for instance, Berkeley and Alvera Mickelsen argue that "head" in 1 Corinthians 11:2–16 means "source" or "origin";[24] but their appeal is to the standard classical lexicon (LSJ—which does of course move forward to cover Hellenistic sources), not the standard New Testament and Hellenistic Greek lexicon (Bauer). The latter lists no meaning of "source" or "origin" for κεφαλή (*kephalē*, head) for the New Testament period.

4. Appeal to unknown or unlikely meanings

We may usefully continue with the previous example. Not only do the Mickelsens appeal to LSJ, but they also fail to note the constraints that even LSJ imposes on the evidence. The Mickelsens make much of the idea *head of a river* as the river's "source"; but in all such cases cited by LSJ, the word is plural, κεφαλαί (*kephalai*). When the singular form κεφαλή (*kephalē*) is applied to a river, it refers to a river's mouth. The only example listed by LSJ where κεφαλή (*kephalē*, sing.) means "source" or "origin" is the document the *Fragmenta Orphilcorum*, from the fifth century B.C. or earlier, which is both textually uncertain and patient of more than one translation.[25] Although some of the New Testament metaphorical uses of κεφαλή (*kephalē*) could be taken to mean "source," all other factors being equal, in no case is that the required meaning; and in every instance the notion of "headship" implying authority fits equally well or better. The relevant lexica are full of examples, all culled from the ancient texts, in which κεφαλή (*kephalē*) connotes "authority." The Mickelsens' argument, and that of many others who have

24. Berkeley and Alvera Mickelsen, "The 'Head' of the Epistles," *CT* 25/4 (Feb. 20, 1981): 20–23.

25. This information was brought to my attention by my colleague, Wayne A. Grudem, in a review in *Trinity Journal* 3 (1982): 230.

joined the same refrain, probably depends on an article by S. Bedale;[26] but the fact remains that whatever the dependencies, the Mickelsens are attempting to appeal to an unknown or unlikely meaning. Certainly there are sound exegetical reasons why such a meaning will not fit the context of 1 Corinthians 11:2–16.[27]

There are many examples of this fourth fallacy. Some spring from poor research, perhaps dependence on others without checking the primary sources; others spring from the desire to make a certain interpretation work out, and the interpreter forsakes evenhandedness. In some instances an intrinsically unlikely or ill-attested meaning receives detailed defense and may even become entrenched in the church. For instance, although no less a Pauline scholar than C. E. B. Cranfield has argued that νόμος (*nomos*) sometimes means not Mosaic law or the Mosaic law covenant, but legalism (e.g., Rom. 3:21),[28] the fact remains that the primary defense of that position is not rigorous linguistic evidence but the adoption of a certain structure of relationships between the Old Testament and the New.[29]

Again, Walter C. Kaiser, Jr., has argued more than once that νόμος (*nomos*) in 1 Corinthians 14:34–35 refers not to Mosaic law but to rabbinic interpretation, rabbinic rules that Paul has come to reject.[30] Women are not allowed to speak, but must be in submission, as the νόμος (*nomos*) says. The Old Testament does not say this, Kaiser argues, so Paul must be referring to rabbinic rules. Then in verse 36 Paul fires his own comeback:

26. S. Bedale, "The Meaning of κεφαλή in the Pauline Epistles," *JTS* 5 (1954): 211–15. The quantitity of literature on κεφαλή *(kephalē)* during the past decade has been prodigious. The best brief summary of the debate, with conclusions in line with what I have argued above, is provided by Joseph A. Fitzmyer, "*Kephale* in I Corinthians 11:3," *Interpretation* 47 (1993): 53–59.

27. See especially James B. Hurley, *Man and Woman in Biblical Perspective* (Grand Rapids: Zondervan, 1981), 163–68.

28. C. E. B. Cranfield, "St. Paul and the Law," *SJT* 17 (1964): 43–68.

29. Refer to Douglas J. Moo, "'Law,' 'Works of the Law,' and Legalism in Paul," *WTJ* 45 (1983): 73–100. For discussion of many of the related issues, see D. A. Carson, ed., *From Sabbath to Lord's Day: A Biblical, Historical and Theological Investigation* (Grand Rapids: Zondervan, 1982).

30. Walter C. Kaiser, Jr., "Paul, Women, and the Church," *Worldwide Challenge* 3 (1976): 9–12; *Toward an Exegetical Theology: Biblical Exegesis for Preaching and Teaching* (Grand Rapids: Baker, 1981), 76–77, 118–19.

Did the word of God originate with you, or are you men (μόνους [*monous*], not μόνας [*monas*]) the only ones it reached? Paul, in other words, gives the gist of the opponents' argument, as he does elsewhere in this epistle (e.g., 6:12; 7:1–2), and then gives his own correction. The result is that the passage on the submission of women is a summary of the erroneous views Paul seeks to refute.

This interpretation has its attractions, but it will not stand up to close scrutiny.

Elsewhere in this epistle when Paul rebuts or modifies certain erroneous positions, he never does so with a mere rhetorical question: he argues his case and sketches in an alternative framework of understanding. This observation calls in question the suggestion that all of 14:34–35 can be dismissed by the question of 14:36. The recurring pattern does not *prove* that 14:34–35 could not be introducing a different structure, but since there is no other clear example of this alternative, the observation cannot be lightly dismissed or ignored.

The masculine μόνους (*monous*) in 14:36 does not prove that Paul is addressing only the men of the congregation and asking if they think they are the only ones the word of God has reached—they alone, and not the women. Rather, it refers to both the men and the women who constitute the church: the Greek regularly uses plural masculine forms when people (without distinction as to sex) are being referred to or addressed. This means that Paul by his rhetorical question is rebuking the entire church for its laxness on the issue at hand; he is rebuking the highhandedness its members display on all kinds of issues, a highhandedness that prompts them to break with the practice of other churches and even question Paul's authority. This interpretation of μόνους (*monous*) is confirmed by three things. First, it makes sense of 14:33b, "as in all the congregations of the saints" (NIV): that is, Paul is refuting a practice that sets the Corinthian church off from other churches. (It is syntactically unlikely that 14:33b should be read with 14:33a; rather, it begins the pericope under debate.) Second, this interpretation also suits 14:37–38: apparently the Corinthian believers are so arrogant, so puffed up with an awareness of the spiritual gifts distributed among them, that they are in danger of ignoring apostolic authority. Are they the *only* ones who think they have prophetic gifts? Real spiritual giftedness will recognize that what Paul writes is the Lord's command. The contrast in verse 36, carried on in verses 37–38, is thus not between Corinthian men believers and Corinthian women believers, but between Corinthian believers, men and women, who set themselves over against other churches (14:33b) and even over against apostolic authority (14:37–38). The Corinthians must learn that they are not the *only people* (μόνους [*monous*]) the word of God has reached. And third, this interpretation is confirmed by other passages in this epistle where the same sort of argument is constructed (see especially 7:40b; 11:16).

If verse 36 is not a dismissal of rabbinic tradition, then νόμος (*nomos*) ("as the *Law* says," v. 34, NIV, italics added) cannot refer to that tradition. Now we come to the heart of the fallacy under consideration. Insofar as νόμος (*nomos*) can be a rough Greek equivalent for "Torah," and "Torah" can in rabbinic usage encompass both written Scripture and the oral tradition, a plausible a priori case can be made for understanding νόμος (*nomos*) in verse 34 in this way. But the fact remains that Paul never uses νόμος (*nomos*) in this way anywhere else, even though the word is common in his writings; and therefore to that extent Kaiser's interpretation of this passage, in addition to its other weaknesses, falls under this fourth fallacy. It is an appeal to a meaning unlikely for Paul, if we are to judge by his own usage. The only time such a highly unlikely appeal is justified occurs when other interpretations of the passage are so exegetically unlikely that we are forced to offer some fresh hypothesis. But when this takes place, we need to admit how tentative and linguistically uncertain the theory really is.

In this case, however, there is no need for such a procedure of last resort. The passage can be and has been adequately explained in its context. There are ample parallels to this way of looking to the Old Testament for a principle, not a quotation (and the principle in question is doubtless Gen. 2:20b–24, referred to by Paul both in 1 Cor. 11:8–9 and in 1 Tim. 2:13); and the demand for silence on the part of women does not bring on irreconcilable conflict with 1 Corinthians 11:2–16, where under certain conditions women are permitted to pray and prophesy, because the silence of 14:33b–36 is limited by context: women are to keep silent in connection with the evaluation of prophecies, to which the context refers, for otherwise they would be assuming a role of doctrinal authority in the congregation (contra 1 Tim. 2:11–15).[31]

All of this is to show nothing more than that this fourth fallacy may be obscured by considerable exegetical ingenuity; but it remains a fallacy just the same.

5. Careless appeal to background material

In a sense, the example of the Mickelsens falls under this fallacy as well; but the borders of this fifth fallacy, although they overlap with the fourth, are somewhat broader. There may be an inappropriate appeal to background material that does not involve an intrinsically unlikely meaning.

Since in the previous entry I focused on an example from the writings of a respected former academic dean, Walt Kaiser, I shall now try to make amends, or at least demonstrate a certain evenhandedness, by illustrating this fifth fallacy from my own published works.

The first concerns the words ὕδατος καί (*hydatos kai*) in John 3:5: "I tell you the truth, unless a man is born of *water* and the *Spirit*, he cannot enter the kingdom of God." The interpretations given to those two words are legion, and I do not have space to canvass them here. But after weighing as carefully as I could all the options of which I knew anything, I rejected the various sacramental interpretations on the grounds that they were anachronistic, contextually improbable, and out of synchronization with John's themes. I also rejected various metaphorical interpretations (e.g., water is a symbol for the Word of God—which makes little contextual sense out of the dialogue). In due course I turned away from the view that the water is simply the amniotic fluid that flows away during the process of birth, because I could find no ancient text that spoke of birth as "out of water"— just as we do not speak that way today. With some reluctance, therefore, I followed Hugo Odeberg and Morris, who point to various sources in which "water" or "rain" or "dew" dignifies

31. See especially Hurley, *Man and Woman in Biblical Perspective*, 185–94. Also consult Wayne A. Grudem, *The Gift of Prophecy in 1 Corinthians* (Washington, D.C.: University Press of America, 1982), 239–55; reviewed in *Trinity Journal* 3 (1982): 226–32.

male semen.[32] Understanding γεννάω (*gennaō*) in this passage to
mean "to beget" rather than "to give birth to," John 3:5 then
reads, "Unless a man is begotten of water [=semen; i.e., natural
begetting] and of the spirit [i.e., supernatural begetting], he cannot enter the kingdom of God."
  In fact, the parallels are not good; but my hesitant endorse-
ment of this position[33] has now been shown to be both unconvincing and unnecessary. The person who convinced me was
Linda L. Belleville, one of my graduate students before she went
on to the University of Toronto for doctoral study. The relevant
part of her thesis has been published as an article.[34] She surveys
and interacts with all the published interpretations, including
very recent ones, and argues that ἐξ ὕδατος καὶ πνεύματος (*ex
hydatos kai pneumatos*, of water and spirit), far from referring
to two births, refers to one (the fact that both nouns are gov-
erned by one preposition certainly favors this view). This makes
verses 3, 5, 6b, and 7 all parallel statements. Water and spirit are
already linked in Ezekiel 36:25–27—the prophet foresees a time
of eschatological cleansing in which God will sprinkle clean
water on his people, making them clean (the eschatological
counterpart to the levitical purification rites), and will give them
a new heart and a new spirit. This Nicodemus should have
understood (John 3:10). Birth or begetting "of water and spirit"
is thus not a hendiadys, but a reference to the dual work of the
Spirit (3:6) who simultaneously purifies and imparts God's
nature to man. Belleville's work will stand up to close scrutiny.[35]
  The second example is from my popular-level exposition on
the Sermon on the Mount. I there explained the well-known discrepancy between Matthew's reference to a mountain (5:1) and
Luke's mention of a plain (6:17) with more or less standard conservative apologetic: even a mountain has level places, and so

  32. Hugo Odeberg, *The Fourth Gospel* (1929; Amsterdam: Gruñer, 1968),
48–71; Leon Morris, *The Gospel According to John*, New International Commentary on the New Testament series (Grand Rapids: Eerdmans, 1971), 216–18.
  33. In my doctoral dissertation, "Predestination and Responsibility," Cambridge University, 1975.
  34. Linda L. Belleville, "'Born of Water and Spirit': John 3:5," *Trinity Journal* 1 (1980): 125–40.
  35. I have defended this interpretation at much greater length in my commentary *The Gospel According to John* (Grand Rapids: William B. Eerdmans
Publishing Company, 1991), in loc.

forth.[36] Since publishing that book, however, I have written a full-length technical commentary on Matthew; and I have learned that εἰς τὸ ὄρος (*eis to oros*) in Matthew 5:1 probably does not mean Jesus went "up a mountain" or "to a mountain" or "onto a mountainside," but simply "into the hill country"; and interestingly πεδινός (*pedinos*) in Luke 6:17, usually rendered "plain," commonly refers to a plateau in mountainous regions.[37] There is no discrepancy; I had simply not done enough work for the earlier book. If it is any encouragement, increasing years make one increasingly careful. They are also teaching me, slowly, to change my mind and acknowledge when I am shown to be in error. There is no virtue in a Maginot Line of emotional defense around a position that is palpably weak.

6. Verbal parallelomania

Samuel Sandmel coined the term *parallelomania* to refer to the penchant of many biblical scholars to adduce "parallels" of questionable worth.[38] One subset of such an abuse is verbal parallelomania—the listing of verbal parallels in some body of literature as if those bare phenomena demonstrate conceptual links or even dependency. In an earlier essay[39] I reported the astonishing study by Robert Kysar,[40] who surveyed the use of parallels in the examination of the Johannine prologue (John 1:1–18) as undertaken by C. H. Dodd and Rudolf Bultmann. Of the three hundred or so parallels that each of the two scholars adduced, the overlap was only 7 percent! That 7 percent, I repeat, covers overlap in what was adduced, not in what was deemed significant as background. With so little overlap, one can only conclude that neither scholar had come close to a comprehensive survey of potential backgrounds. One sees a back-

36. D. A. Carson, *The Sermon on the Mount: An Evangelical Exposition of Matthew 5–7* (Grand Rapids: Baker, 1978), 145.

37. D. A. Carson, "Matthew," in *the Expositor's Bible Commentary*, ed. Frank E. Gaebelein (Grand Rapids: Zondervan, 1984), where the evidence is summarized in loc.

38. Samuel Sandmel, "Parallelomania," *JBL* 81 (1962): 2–13.

39. D. A. Carson, "Historical Tradition in the Fourth Gospel: After Dodd, What?" in *Gospel Perspectives* II, ed. R. T. France and David Wenham (Sheffield: JSOT Press, 1981), 101–2.

40. Robert Kysar, "The Background of the Prologue of the Fourth Gospel: A Critique of Historical Methods," *CanJTh* 16 (1970): 250–55.

ground in the Mandaean literature, the other in the Hermetica. Both of these backgrounds are dubious even on the grounds of the dating of the sources; yet both scholars proceed to ascribe to the words of John's prologue the meanings of similar or identical words in fundamentally different corpora. Neither scholar exhibits much linguistic sensitivity to the need for contrastive paradigmatic equivalence or, more broadly, for equivalent contracts in the semantic fields of the texts being compared. I shall refer to these problems again (fallacy 16); suffice it to say here that Arthur Gibson, for instance, is rightly very harsh on Bultmann in this respect.[41]

7. Linkage of language and mentality

It was not long ago that this fallacy generated many books. If one mentions titles like *Hebrew Thought Compared with Greek*[42] in a room full of linguistically competent people, there will instantly be many pained expressions and groans. The heart of this fallacy is the assumption that any language so constrains the thinking processes of the people who use it that they are forced into certain patterns of thought and shielded from others. Language and mentality thus become confused. The *Theological Dictionary of the New Testament* was particularly guilty of this linkage; and it was to Barr's great credit that he exposed its bankruptcy, not only in his work on biblical language,[43] but also in his narrower study comparing concepts of time in Hebrew and Greek thought.[44] This point has been made so often in recent years, and the problem has been so conveniently summarized by Silva,[45] that perhaps I need not say much more about it here. But one should be suspicious of all statements about the nature of "the Hebrew mind" or "the Greek mind" if those statements are based on observations about the semantic limitations of words of the language in question.

Silva cites a deliciously painful example from a conservative textbook, which says that Hebrew has a certain "biographical

41. Gibson, *Biblical Semantic Logic*, 53–54.
42. T. Bowman, *Hebrew Thought Compared with Greek* (London: SCM, 1960).
43. Barr, *The Semantics of Biblical Language*.
44. James Barr, *Biblical Words for Time* (London: SCM, 1969).
45. Silva, *Biblical Words and Their Meaning*, 18–34.

suitability" and quotes approvingly the judgment that "the Hebrew thought in pictures, and consequently his nouns are concrete and vivid. There is no such thing as neuter gender, for the Semite everything is alive."[46] One wonders if neuter entities in other languages must be dead—τὸ παιδίον (*to paidion*), for instance, or *das Mädchen*.

When I was a student at seminary, I was told, in all seriousness, that Greek was an eminently suitable language for the Lord to use in providing New Testament revelation, since, unlike Hebrew, it has a past, a present, and a future tense, and was therefore better able to deal with the temporal location of New Testament revelation. New Testament writers needed to be able to look back to what God had revealed in the *past*, grasp what God was going to do in the *present*, and anticipate what God was going to do in the *future*. But did not the covenant community in Isaiah's day have similar needs? Were the ancient Hebrews unable to distinguish past, present, and future because their language has only two aspects?

8. False assumptions about technical meaning

In this fallacy, an interpreter falsely assumes that a word always or nearly always has a certain technical meaning—a meaning usually derived either from a subset of the evidence or from the interpreter's personal systematic theology. An easy example is the word *sanctification*. In most conservative theological discussion, sanctification is the progressive purifying of the believer, the process by which he becomes increasingly holy after an instantaneous "positional" or "forensic" justification. But it is a commonplace among Pauline scholars that although the term *sanctification* can have that force, it commonly refers to the initial setting aside of an individual for God at his conversion. Thus Paul can address his first epistle to the Corinthians, that singularly "unholy" church, to those who have been sanctified in Christ Jesus (ἡγιασμένοις ἐν Χριστῷ Ἰησοῦ [*hēgiasmenois en Christō Iesou*], 1 Cor. 1:2).

That one, of course, is well known; but there are many others. If ἀποκαλύπτω (*apokalyptō*, to reveal) is thought to refer

---

46. Ibid., 21 citing Norman L. Geisler and William E. Nix, *A General Introduction to the Bible* (Chicago: Moody, 1968), 219.

invariably to special revelation hitherto unknown, the interpreter is going to have difficulty with Philippians 3:15b ("And if
on some point you think differently, that too God will *make clear
to you*"; NIV, italics added). Or how about "baptism in the
Spirit"? Charismatics tend to want to make all occurrences of
the expression refer to a postconversion effusion of Spirit;[47]
some anticharismatics contemplate 1 Corinthians 12:13 ("For
we were all baptized by one Spirit into one body—whether Jews
or Greeks, slave or free—and we were all given one Spirit to
drink," NIV) and conclude, with equal fallacy, that all New Testament references are to the effusion of Spirit all Christians
receive at their conversion.[48] The problem is complicated by the
uncertain syntax of 1 Corinthians 12:13;[49] but the worst problem is the assumption on both sides that we are dealing with a
terminus technicus that always has the same meaning. There is
insufficient evidence to support that view; and the assumption
makes it exceedingly difficult to handle the five passages (one in
each Gospel and one in Acts) that stand in most urgent need of
being treated carefully and evenhandedly as references to a step
in the progress of redemption. Interestingly, the Puritans
adopted neither extreme. Apparently detecting in the phrase
baptism in Holy Spirit no consistent, technical meaning, they
took it to mean "effusion in Spirit" or "inundation in Spirit" and
felt free to pray for revival in the terms, "Oh, baptize us afresh
with thy Holy Spirit!"[50]

Sometimes the detection of an alleged *terminus technicus* is
bound up with distinguishable but complex arguments. For
example, several scholars have argued that in the Great Com-
mission (Matt. 28:18–20), the phrase πάντα τὰ ἔθνη (*panta ta*

47. See the discussion and sources in Walter J. Hollenweger, *The Pentecos-
tals* (London: SCM, 1972), 330–41.
48. See the important discussion and references in Frederick Dale Bruner,
A Theology of the Holy Spirit (Grand Rapids: Eerdmans, 1970), passim.
49. If ἐν ἑνὶ πνεύματι (*en eni pneumati*) is given instrumental force, then in
this passage alone we read that the Holy Spirit baptizes us into one body, whereas in the other New Testament passages (Matt. 3:11; Mark 1:8; Luke 3:16; John
1:33; Acts 1:5 [in connection with Acts 2]) we learn that Jesus baptizes his followers in or with the Holy Spirit. On this basis, some try to distinguish two separate works of grace.
50. See Iain Murray, "Baptism with the Spirit: What Is the Scriptural Meaning?" *Banner of Truth Magazine* 127 (April 1974): 5–22.

ethnē, all nations) excludes Israel.[51] After all, τὰ ἔθνη (*ta ethnē*) in its eight occurrences in Matthew (4:15; 6:32; 10:5, 18; 12:18, 21; 20:19, 25) normally denotes Gentiles, usually pagans, and, it is argued, this interpretation not only makes sense of this technical force in τὰ ἔθνη (*ta ethnē*) but also meshes with Matthew's argument that Israel has forfeited her place, so that the preaching of the gospel must now be kept from her.

Despite its superficial plausibility, the argument has several weaknesses, not least the fact that it stumbles on this eighth fallacy. It is doubtful, for instance, that ἔθνος (*ethnos*), used anarthrously, has this exclusive force in 21:43; and when the entire expression (πάντα τὰ ἔθνη [*panta ta ethnē*], "all nations"—not just τὰ ἔθνη [*ta ethnē*]) occurs in Matthew (24:9, 14; 25:32; 28:19) it is very doubtful that Jews are being excluded. After all, could Jesus really be excluding Israel as one source of the opposition and hate his followers will have to endure (24:9)? Many other arguments could be advanced;[52] but the heart of the problem is the unjustified adoption of a too restrictive *terminus technicus*.

One corollary of this fallacy is that some interpreters will go one stage further and reduce an entire doctrine to one word which they have understood to be a technical term. This is true, for instance, of many treatments of the verb *to foreknow*. But as I have discussed this problem elsewhere, I shall refrain from probing it again.[53]

9. Problems surrounding synonyms and componential analysis

There are two principal and related fallacies I would like to bring up under this heading. The first arises from the fact that the terms *synonymy* and *equivalence* are so little understood by many of us that adequate distinctions are not always preserved.

51. D. R. A. Hare, *The Theme of Jewish Persecution of Christians in the Gospel According to St. Matthew* (Cambridge: University Press, 1967), 147–48; Rolf Walker, *Die Heilsgeschichte im Ersten Evangelium* (Göttingen: Vandenhoeck und Ruprecht, 1967), 111–13; D. R. A. Hare and D. J. Harrington, "'Make Disciples of All the Gentiles' (Mt. 28:19)," *CBQ* 37 (1975): 359–69.

52. For fuller treatment and bibliography, see D. A. Carson, "Matthew," in the *Expositor's Bible Commentary*, in loc.

53. D. A. Carson, *Divine Sovereignty and Human Responsibility: Biblical Perspectives in Tension*, ed. Peter Toon and Ralph Martin (Grand Rapids: Baker Book House, repr. 1994), especially 3–4.

In J. T. Sanders's treatment of Philippians 2:6–11, for instance, he establishes the stanza division to his own satisfaction, and then says, "The second line in either case then explicates what was said in the first line; this is done synonymously in the second stanza ('likeness' = 'fashion', 'of men' = 'like a man'). . . . 'Humbled himself' is the equivalent . . . to 'emptied himself.'"[54] Gibson analyzes the problem.[55] Strictly speaking, "explicates" is incompatible with "synonymously" and perhaps with "equivalent"; for to the extent that two items are synonymous neither can explicate the other. The two items would have the same semantic value. Incidentally, although Gibson does not mention it, this is a major problem in most treatments of Hebrew poetry. Many scholars treat lexical units in Semitic poetry as synonymous, others as very rough "synonyms" that shed light on each other, and some confuse the two. It is arguable that the habits of Hebrew poets are diverse enough to admit both strict synonymy and explication in most poems, but not at the same time in the same pair of items![56] Also, the parallels Sanders draws are not exactly synonymous. Even "of men"/"like a man" "are semantically asymmetrical regarding 'of' and 'like' and *quantificationally distinct in men/man;* so it is, at the most, only at some levels that the equated components share semantic levels, with differences at others, while Sanders distinguishes neither group."[57] Third, the equations Sanders advances could in theory be reconstructed as hyponymic relations (i.e., the pairs of items do not have the same semantic values: they do not mean exactly the same things, but they have the same referents [they make reference to the same realities, even though their meaning is different]).[58] Unfortunately, Sanders does not see his equations that way.

54. J. T. Sanders, *The New Testament Christological Hymns* (Cambridge: University Press, 1971), 10.

55. Gibson, *Biblical Semantic Logic*, 45–46.

56. The standard Old Testament introductions treat these matters in a cursory fashion, but recent journal literature boasts many fresh studies on parallelism in Hebrew poetry.

57. Gibson, *Biblical Semantic Logic*, 45.

58. Following Gibson's lead, the label *hyponymic* in this context springs from John Lyons, *Introduction to Theoretical Linguistics* (Cambridge: University Press, 1968), especially 453–60. For extended discussion of problems of synonymy, see Ullmann, *Semantics*, 141–55.

FIGURE 1

	Entries			
	man	**woman**	**boy**	**girl**
human	+	+	+	+
adult	+	+	-	-
male	+	-	+	-

(left label: **Components of Meaning**)

The point of this rather painful exercise is not to denigrate the work of a biblical scholar, since one could argue, for instance, that Sanders does not mean to take "synonymously" in the same rigorous way that modern linguists demand. He might be a "layman" as far as linguistic theory is concerned, and therefore permitted to use terms like "synonyms" in a nontechnical way. But that is just the problem, for the theological agenda is illegitimately controlling the equations, flattening semantic distinctions, violating levels of meaning by squashing them into one equation, with the result that the text cannot speak with all its force, with its full semantic power. The fallacy is the unwarranted belief that "synonyms" are identical in more ways than the evidence allows.

To present the second problem, I must say a little about componential analysis. This kind of study attempts to isolate the components of meaning (i.e., the semantic components) of (usually) words. Figure 1 provides a frequently repeated example. The chart is self-explanatory. But notice that the semantic components (human, adult, male) do not exhaust the possible constituents of meaning that could go into "man." To make matters worse, most linguists permit only those semantic components that are referents: that is, componential analysis is applicable only to referential meaning, not to what the word means in a particular context but to all that it refers.[59] In the

59. I shall return to this question in point 16. See especially Eugene A. Nida, *Componential Analysis of Meaning* (The Hague: Mouton, 1974); and, more briefly, Silva, *Biblical Words and Their Meaning*, 132–35.

case of many words, the list of semantic "components" becomes very long and cumbersome indeed. Moreover, there is no agreed procedure for analyzing terms componentially, and therefore different scholars sometimes achieve quite different results—which is not very reassuring. But even where two analyses of a term agree, they do not usually claim to list all of the elements that go into the meaning of the term under scrutiny, since componential analysis normally provides only the elements of referential meaning.

Perhaps it will now be a little clearer why synonyms are so difficult to handle. In one sense, of course, two terms are virtually never strictly synonymous if by "synonymous" we are saying that *wherever they are used* the two terms mean exactly the same thing denotatively and connotatively, in their semantic components and in the cognitive information they convey and in the emotional freight they carry, to all people who speak the language. But a pair of words can be strictly synonymous in certain contexts; each case must be decided on its own merits. To illustrate with another commonly used diagram, figure 2, the terms A and B may be strictly synonymous in a particular context where they enjoy semantic overlap (i.e., overlapping meanings, indicated by the shaded area). For strict synonymy, of course, the semantic overlap must include not only referential meaning, but also all the aspects that go into meaning; for otherwise the terms A and B are "synonymous" at some levels and not at others.

FIGURE 2

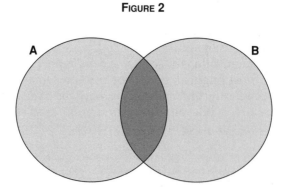

We are now equipped to resume our discussion of ἀγαπάω (*agapaō*) and φιλέω (*phileō*), introduced in the discussion about the root fallacy. There we saw that ἀγαπάω (*agapaō*) does not always refer to a "good" love or a sacrificial love or a divine love, and certainly there is nothing in the root to convey such a meaning. But the question arises whether the well-known exchange between Jesus and Peter reported in John 21:15–17, using the two different verbs, is intended to convey a distinction in meaning, or to provide an example of semantic overlap, of synonymy. The pattern is shown in figure 3.

FIGURE 3

Jesus' question	Peter's response
ἀγαπάω	φιλέω
ἀγαπάω	φιλέω
φιλέω	φιλέω

For various reasons, I doubt very much that there is an intended distinction. If I were setting out to prove the point, I would have to discuss the significance of "the third time," exegete the passage in some detail, review the evidence that John regularly introduces expressions that are either precisely synonymous or roughly so,[60] and so forth. But most of those who insist that there is a distinction to be made in John's use of the two verbs do so on one of two grounds. First, they argue that translators of the Septuagint and New Testament writers have invested[61] ἀγαπάω (*agapaō*, to love) and ἀγάπη (*agapē*, love) with special meaning to provide an adequate expression by which to talk about the love of God; and only this accounts for the word's rapid rise to prominence in our literature. But this argument has been overturned by the diachronic study of Robert Joly, who presents convincing evidence that ἀγαπάω (*aga-*

60. Refer to Leon Morris, *Studies in the Fourth Gospel* (Grand Rapids: Eerdmans, 1969), 293–319.
61. The less sophisticated, of course, will not use the word *invested*, but will say that the writers of the Septuagint and the New Testament *chose* ἀγαπάω (*agapaō*) and cognates as the only adequate term with which to talk about God's love. But this is a return to the root fallacy, already discussed.

paō) was coming into prominence throughout Greek literature from the fourth century B.C. on, and was not restricted to biblical literature.[62] This development was fostered by a number of changes in the language (linguists call them structural changes) in which ἀγαπάω (*agapaō*) was becoming one of the standard verbs for "to love" because φιλέω (*phileō*) had acquired the meaning *to kiss* as part of *its* semantic range. The reasons for these developments need not detain us;[63] but the evidence is substantial and effectively disqualifies this first ground.

The second ground on which many build their argument that ἀγαπάω (*agapaō*) is to be distinguished from φιλέω (*phileō*) in John 21:15–17—and the one that concerns us most directly at the moment—is well illustrated by William Hendriksen's commentary.[64] Hendriksen shows that although there is considerable semantic overlap between ἀγαπάω (*agapaō*) and φιλέω (*phileō*), once one considers all the biblical passages in which these two words occur there is clear evidence for a little semantic "overhang" in each case. For instance, φιλέω (*phileō*) can be used when Judas kisses Jesus (Luke 22:47); ἀγαπάω (*agapaō*) is never used in such a context. On this sort of basis, then, Hendriksen concludes that ἀγαπάω (*agapaō*) and φιλέω (*phileō*) are not complete synonyms, and therefore that they preserve slightly differently semantic thrusts in John 21:15–17.

Whatever the outcome of the continued debate on this passage, it should by now be obvious that Hendriksen's argument will not stand up, precisely because he mishandles the difficult questions surrounding synonymy. The heart of his argument is that the total semantic range of each word is slightly different from the other, and therefore that there is a semantic differ-

---

62. Robert Joly, *Le vocabulaire chrétien de l'amour est-il original? Φιλεῖν et ἀγαπᾶν dans le grec antique* (Brussels: Presses Universitaires, 1968).

63. Briefly, Joly demonstrates that φιλέω (*phileō*) acquired this new and additional meaning because an older verb for "to kiss," κυνέω (*kyneō*), was dropping out; and the reason for this latter disappearance was the homonymic clash with yet another verb, κύνω (*kynō*, which means "to impregnate"), particularly in the aorist, where both κυνέω (*kyneō*, to kiss) and κύνω (*kynō*, to impregnate) have the same form ἔκυσα (*ekysa*). This would encourage various salacious puns and gradually force κυνέω (*kyneō*) into obsolescence.

64. William Hendriksen, *The Gospel of John*, 2 vols. (Grand Rapids: Baker, 1953–54), especially 2:494–500.

ence in this context. But if we decide contextually specific questions of synonymy on the basis of the total semantic range of each word, any synonymy in any context is virtually impossible. Hendriksen's treatment illegitimately forecloses the question.[65]

This particular example of a confused understanding of synonymy is a special instance of "illegitimate totality transfer," discussed again under fallacy 13. Intriguingly, those who insist on two distinguishable meanings for ἀγαπάω (*agapaō*) and φιλέω (*phileō*) in John 21:15–17 rarely observe that there are other subtle differences in the three sets of exchanges between Jesus and Peter. Note especially the three responses Jesus gives to Peter:

> (v.15) βόσκε τὰ ἀρνία μου (*boske ta arnia mou*, "Feed my lambs")
> (v.16) ποίμαινε τὰ πρόβατά μου (*poimaine ta probata mou*, "Shepherd my sheep")
> (v.17) βόσκε τὰ πρόβατά μου (*boske ta probata mou*, "Feed my sheep")

My somewhat pedantic translation, in parentheses, highlights the changes. But very few preachers judge these changes to be of fundamental importance to the meaning of the passage. One can show that there is some difference between "lambs" and "sheep" when the totality of their respective semantic ranges is taken into account; similarly, there is a difference between "to shepherd" and "to feed." But in this context, it is difficult to see a fundamental theological or linguistic or syntactical reason for the changes. We seem to be in the realm of slight variation for the sake of vague things like "feel" or "style." In any case, my point is that it is rather strange to insist on a semantic distinction between the two words for "to love" *in this context*, and not on small distinctions between other pairs of words in the same context.

65. Perhaps I should add that I am not suggesting there is nothing distinctive about God's love. The Scriptures insist there is. But the content of God's love is not connected on a one-to-one basis with the semantic range of any single word or word group. What the Bible has to say about the love of God is conveyed by sentences, paragraphs, discourses, and so forth; that is, by larger semantic units than the word.

10. Selective and prejudicial use of evidence

We have already come across an instance of this fallacy in describing certain treatments of the word κεφαλή (*kephalē*) (fallacy 4); but in that instance my point was that background material was improperly handled. Now I am describing a slightly different fallacy, one that may have to do with background material, but is certainly not restricted to such material. I am referring to the kind of appeal to selective evidence that enables the interpreter to say what he or she wants to say, without really listening to what the Word of God says.

Examples of this kind of phenomenon are so numerous that a book could easily be compiled of the various types of distortion generated by this fallacy. I shall restrict myself to one example. Thomas H. Groome, a noted Roman Catholic authority on Christian education, in his discussion of "the Biblical way of knowing," falls into several exegetical pitfalls.[66] He is deeply guilty of fallacy 7, confusing language and mentality, when he tries to argue that the Hebrew way of knowing is not intellectual but experiential. Greek thought, he claims, is quite different; but fortunately (for his thesis), the Hebrew background modified normal pagan Greek, so that even in the New Testament "to know God" has to do with experience, obedience, loving others—not with the acquisition of data. He thus manages to run afoul of fallacies connected with the improper relation of the Old Testament Semitic background with the New Testament itself (see point 14), and commits himself to the disjunctive fallacy (11, to which I shall turn next). But my concern at the moment is his selective use of biblical evidence. He turns to John's writings and cites those passages which in some way relate knowing God or believing in God to keeping God's commandments and loving others (e.g., 1 John 2:3–5; 3:6).[67] But he fails to cite those many passages, both in John's writings and elsewhere, that show there is *also* propositional content to Christian belief. For instance, if I may provide some examples

66. Thomas H. Groome, *Christian Religious Education: Sharing Our Story and Vision* (San Francisco: Harper and Row, 1980), especially 141–45. I am grateful to Perry G. Downs for bringing this work to my attention.
67. It is doubtful if Groome really understands the passages he cites, for he betrays no awareness of the manner in which these texts relate to the situations in which they were first penned.

from John, it is imperative to believe not only Christ, but also what he says (e.g., 4:50; 5:47; 11:26); and there are sometimes content clauses after the verb *to believe*—that is, "to believe *that* . . ." (e.g., John 13:19; 17:21). Certainly Christian belief and Christian knowledge are not exclusively intellectual; but by being selective with the evidence, Groome has managed to conclude that Christian belief and knowledge are exclusively experiential and nonintellectual. The result is a theory of education that consistently depreciates content. The fallacy lies in Groome's implicit supposition that the presentation of selective evidence constitutes proof.

11. Unwarranted semantic disjunctions and restrictions

Not a few word studies offer the reader either/or alternatives and then force a decision. In other words, they demand semantic disjunction, when complementarity might be a possibility.

We have just witnessed an example from Groome. Here is another, from one of Groome's colleagues in Christian education. Lawrence O. Richards, arguing that headship in the New Testament has nothing to do with authority (and here his work is a particularly appalling example of the kind of fallacy I discussed in entry 5), comes at last to talking about Jesus' headship of the church:

> Authority, with its right to control and demand obedience, is not suggested. The fact that the living head of the church, Jesus, is a person with supreme authority is presented to comfort and assure it of His ability to meet its needs. . . . As head He is the source and origin of our life. As head He is the one who sustains the whole body and supplies all we need for growth. As head He is the one who has committed Himself to serve us and is able to bring saving transformation to our personalities. He stoops to lift us up.[68]

Here is formidable disjunction indeed! Either Jesus as head is authoritative and has the right to control and demand obedience, or as head he stoops to lift us up! The truth of the matter is that the eternal Son humbled himself to become a man, and

---

68. Lawrence O. Richards and Clyde Hoeldtke, *A Theology of Church Leadership* (Grand Rapids: Zondervan, 1980), 21.

stoops to lift us up, *and* is authoritative and has the right to control things and demand obedience. All authority is his (Matt. 28:18); even our friendship with him is predicated on our obedience to him (John 15:14—which shows that in this sense the friendship is not reciprocal). And these authority themes are directly connected with Jesus' headship.[69] Richards has committed the disjunctive fallacy (as he repeatedly does) and as a result is not listening to Scripture.

Consider R. C. H. Lenski's treatment of Jesus' prayer in John 17:11, "that they may be one, *just* as (καθώς [*kathōs*] we are one."[70] Because Lenski wishes to preserve the distinctive unity of the Trinity, he insists that καθώς (*kathōs*, just as) makes it clear the oneness believers are to enjoy is analogical to that of the Trinity, not identical. Note the form of the argument: either our oneness is analogical, or it is identical; and that it is the former is proved by the presence of καθώς (*kathōs*). I agree doctrinally with Lenski: believers cannot precisely duplicate the oneness that exists among the persons of the Godhead, but in certain respects they can imitate it. The steps Lenski takes to reach this conclusion, however, are invalid. In the first place, a statement may be formally analogical (i.e., it may be constructed in the form "A is *just as* B") yet establish identity of relationships: for example, "A cat is an animal *just as* a dog is an animal." This is formally equivalent to "Christians are one *just as* the Father and Son are one"; but in the statement about animals there is identity of relationship. But in the second place, Lenski compounds his error by restricting the semantic range of καθώς (*kathōs*) so that it can *only* make statements that are analogical (formally *and* ontologically). The fallacy is in failing to grasp the full semantic range of the word καθώς (*kathōs*), which in the New Testament is certainly broad enough to function in *both* of my model sentences.[71] This failure leads to Lenski's erroneous belief that the very presence of καθώς (*kathōs*) justifies his theological conclusion.

---

69. See especially the discussion in Hurley, *Man and Woman in Biblical Perspective*, 163–68.

70. R. C. H. Lenski, *The Interpretation of St. John's Gospel* (Minneapolis: Augsburg, 1936), 1138.

71. For instance, one finds identity of *relationship* despite discontinuities in the analogy in a passage such as John 15:4.

His theological conclusion will stand; but it needs to seek justification elsewhere.

12. Unwarranted restriction of the semantic field

There are many different ways of misunderstanding the meaning of a word in a particular context by illegitimately restricting the word's semantic range. It may be by falsely declaring it a *terminus technicus* (entry 8), by resorting to semantic disjunctions (entry 11), or by abusing background material (entry 5). But the problem transcends these individual categories.

We sometimes fail to appreciate how wide the total semantic range of a word is; therefore when we come to perform the exegesis of a particular passage, we do not adequately consider the potential options and unwittingly exclude possibilities that might include the correct one. A frequently cited example of semantic breadth is bound up with our word *board*.[72] A board is a piece of dressed lumber, a plank. Many people pay room and board, an expression possibly derived from the fact that in older English the table from which one ate on special occasions was called a festive board. A group of people gathered together for business might be called a board of trustees; and if they get on a ship or a train, they will step on board and hope they do not fall overboard. The same word can function as a verb: workmen may board up a broken window, and passengers board a jetliner.

Trying to drive home the point to one of my classes a few years ago, I asked the students to give me a noun, any noun, to see if I could find more than one meaning. The class wag immediately offered "roller coaster." But even in this case, a moment's reflection turned up the fact that someone involved in a romance that is blowing hot and cold may say, "My love life is a roller coaster!" and everyone will understand what is meant. The point is that colorful word metaphors (and new ones are being invented all the time) must also be included in any word's total semantic range.

Few words with broad semantic range cause more interpre-

72. See Milton S. Terry, *Biblical Hermeneutics: A Treatise on the Interpretation of the Old and New Testaments* (1883; Grand Rapids: Zondervan, 1974), 191.

tative difficulties than the copula εἰμί (*eimi*, to be). Caird provides a useful list of what he calls the "main types" of copula usage in Greek:[73]

a. Identity: "Is the law sin?" (Rom. 7:7)
b. Attribute: "No one is good except God alone" (Mark 10:18)
c. Cause: "To be carnally minded is death" (Rom. 8:6)
d. Resemblance: "The tongue is a fire" (James 3:6)

This is very helpful and is obviously pertinent to any consideration of the four most disputed words in the Bible, "This is my body." Several branches of Christendom treat "is" in this sentence as a statement of identity; but quite clearly the semantic range of "to be" is broad enough that identity cannot legitimately be presupposed: it must be argued. Conversely, those who oppose the view that "is" in "this is my body" establishes identity cannot legitimately do so on the ground that neither Hebrew nor Aramaic possesses a true copula;[74] for in the first place, that argument assumes the Semitic languages have so influenced the semantic range of εἰμί (*eimi*) that it too is similarly restricted—an assumption that not only needs proving but also is in fact false, and in the second place the argument assumes Hebrew and Aramaic are incapable of expressing predication by any means, which is also false.

Caird proceeds to argue that the statement *this is my body* cannot be one of identity, because "Jesus cannot be supposed to have identified the bread in his hands with the living body of which those hands were part."[75] But if "body" in this instance has a slightly different referent than the body of which the hands are a part, then "is" is being used metaphorically, and all metaphors belong to class d. The problem, Caird says, is that as soon as we suggest "is" here means something like "represents" or "symbolizes,"

73. Caird, *Language and Imagery*, 101. These uses of εἰμί (*eimi*, to be) are types of copula usage only; in addition the verb can serve to make a statement of existence, for example, "In the beginning *was* the Word" (John 1:1).
74. The Hebrew verb שֵׁי (*yesh*) is used in statements of existence, but is not ordinarily used as a copula, except in the future tense where the sense is close to "become." Consult Caird, *Language and Imagery*, 100.
75. Ibid., 101.

the traditional riposte is that the eucharistic elements are not to be regarded as "mere symbols." The fallacy in this objection lies in the assumption that symbols are invariably substitutes for the reality they signify, bearing the same relation to it as a still-life painting to real fruit and fish, whetting but not satisfying the appetite. But many symbols, such as a kiss, a handshake and the presentation of a latchkey, are a means, or even the means, of conveying what they represent. The most natural way of taking the copula in the eucharistic saying, therefore, is "represents," with the understanding that Jesus intended the gift of bread to convey the reality it symbolized.[76]

All this initially seems convincing; but there is one weakness in this argument. In two of the examples Caird gives, a kiss is a symbol of love that actually conveys love because it is part of love; a latchkey given to a growing child is a symbol of freedom that actually conveys freedom because it is one of the means of that freedom. But bread is not simultaneously a symbol for and a part of Jesus' body in the same way a kiss is a symbol for and a part of love. Caird's example of a handshake is slightly better; but my point in raising these hesitations is to show that even when "is" is correctly identified as to type of copula, all further discussion is not thereby foreclosed.

We turn now to reflect on Caird's second discussion arising from the four uses of the copula. The final clause of John 1:1, "the Word was God," looks like a statement of identity; but, Caird insists, this cannot be, because the second clause ("the Word was with God") denies it. If we try to take "the Word was God" as an attributive statement (type b—so NEB's "what God was, the Word was"), we still have a problem; for "since God is a class of one, whoever has all the attributes of God is God, so that the attributive converts into a statement of identity."[77] Caird is ultimately forced to propose a tentative and very paraphrastic rendering that in fact arouses a host of new questions; but the problem is of his own making. Statements of identity are not necessarily reciprocal: "a dog is an animal" does not imply "an animal is a dog." Thus "the Word was God" does not imply "God was the Word." It is true that whoever has the attributes of God must be God; but if that person who has the attributes of

76. Ibid., 101–2.
77. Ibid., 102.

God also has some other attributes, we cannot say God is also that person. Caird simply *affirms* that the second clause of John 1:1 disallows the view that the third clause is an identity statement; but that affirmation is demanded by neither lexical semantics nor syntax. The fourth evangelist certainly gives the impression that although God is one, he is some kind of plural unity; for he does not hesitate to have the incarnate Word addressed as Lord and God (20:28).[78] That same perspective may permit us to let the second and third clauses of John 1:1 stand side by side without embarrassment.

In addition to these four standard types of copula usage, I want to add a fifth:

e. Fulfillment: "This is what was spoken by the prophet" (Acts 2:16, NIV).

This is not an identity statement, since the antecedent of "this" is the set of phenomena associated with that first Christian Pentecost, not the prophecy itself. The statement really means, "This fulfills what was spoken by the prophet." The same is likely true of the Golden Rule (Matt. 7:12). The Golden Rule "is" the Law and the Prophets; but since this cannot be an identity statement, some have taken it as type d. It is contextually superior to take it as type e: the Golden Rule fulfills the Law and the Prophets, which are presented in Matthew as having a prophetic role in both proposition and type (see 5:17–20; 11:11–13).[79]

Be this as it may, my point is that the unwarranted and premature restriction of the semantic field of a word is a methodological error. The fallacy lies in thinking the correct interpretation of a passage can be discovered anyway; and in many instances that is not possible.

13. Unwarranted adoption of an expanded semantic field

The fallacy in this instance lies in the supposition that the meaning of a word in a specific context is much broader than the context itself allows and may bring with it the word's entire semantic range. This step is sometimes called illegitimate total-

---

78. Refer to the extended discussion of this aspect of Johannine Christology in Carson, *Divine-Sovereignty and Human Responsibility*, 146–60.

79. See Carson, Matthew, in the *Expositor's Bible Commentary*, in loc.

ity transfer. I presented one example of this danger, a rather special case, in the discussion of problems surrounding synonymy (entry 9). Silva describes many more.[80] Of these I pass on one: "It would be admittedly invalid to overload Acts 7:38 with all the senses in which ἐκκλησία [*ekklēsia*, "church"] is used by the apostles; some of these senses (e.g., reference to the so-called universal church) would actually be contradictory in this verse. However, it is easy, especially in the course of a sermon, to comment on the broad meanings of a word at the risk of obscuring its specific function in a given text."[81]

14. Problems relating to the Semitic background of the Greek New Testament

There is a large nest of difficult questions that can be grouped together under this heading, and a corresponding array of fallacies. The kinds of problems I have in mind may be brought out by asking a few rhetorical questions: To what extent is the vocabulary of the Greek New Testament shaped by the Semitic languages which, presumably, underlie large parts of it (especially the Gospels and parts of Acts)? To what extent are the normal semantic ranges of New Testament Greek words altered by the impact of the writer? Or by his reading of the Hebrew Old Testament, where applicable? Or by the indirect influence of the Hebrew Old Testament on the Septuagint, which has in turn influenced the New Testament?

Many similar questions could be raised; but this chapter, already too long, must be drawn to a close. The need for substantial discussion has been diminished by the recent work of Silva,[82] who ably points out the weaknesses in Edwin Hatch's method,[83] which sought to establish the meanings of Greek words by simple recourse to their Hebrew equivalents—a method sadly given a new lease on life by Nigel Turner.[84] This is

---

80. Silva, *Biblical Words and Their Meaning*, 25–27.

81. Ibid., 25–26.

82. Ibid., 53–73; "Bilingualism and the Character of New Testament Greek," *Bib* 69 (1980): 198–219.

83. Edwin Hatch, *Essays in Biblical Greek* (Oxford: Clarendon, 1889), especially 11ff.

84. Nigel Turner, *Christian Words* (Edinburgh: T. and T. Clark, 1980). See the important review by Moisés Silva in *Trinity Journal* 3 (1982): 103–9.

not to say that the Septuagint had no influence on New Testament writers. Far from it: the influence was profound. But it is to say that it is methodologically irresponsible to read the meaning of a Hebrew word into its Greek equivalent without further ado. The case must be argued. For instance, one must ask the prior question about the degree to which the Septuagint (let alone the New Testament) invested Greek words with Hebrew meanings. Although it is true that words only partially overlap between languages, nevertheless "all languages can talk about the same meaning, and for that matter about all meanings."[85] It is just that receptor languages may have to use entirely different constructions, or resort to periphrasis, or exercise care in selecting words that have just the *right* semantic overlap with the words of the donor language. Thus all along in the study of words in the Septuagint, it is necessary *both* to examine the intention of the original Hebrew *and* to study Hellenistic literature and papyri to be reasonably knowledgeable about the semantic range of Greek words current in the days of the translators of the Septuagint. These considerations are circumvented when a scholar moves directly from the semantic range of a Hebrew word in the Old Testament to that of a Greek word in the New Testament.

15. Unwarranted neglect of distinguishing peculiarities of a corpus

Because Paul uses δικαιόω (*dikaioō*) to mean "to justify," and often uses δικαιοσύνη (*dikaiosynē*) to mean "justification," many scholars have applied this meaning to the term when it is used by other writers. Not a few, for instance, take "justification" to be the meaning of δικαιοσύνη (*dikaiosynē*) in Matthew 5:20; but Benno Przybylski has convincingly shown that δικαιοσύνη (*dikaiosynē*) in Matthew always means an individual's conduct of righteous life, not forensic righteousness imputed to him.[86] Again, the "call" of God in Paul is effective: if someone is "called," he is a believer. By contrast, in the synoptic Gospels, the "call" of God means something like God's "invitation," for in

---

85. Louw, *Semantics of New Testament Greek*, 45.
86. Benno Przybylski, *Righteousness in Matthew and His World of Thought* (Cambridge: University Press, 1980).

these writers' usage many are "called" but few are chosen (Matt. 20:16; 22:14). The fallacy involved in this case is the false assumption that one New Testament writer's predominant usage of any word is roughly that of all other New Testament writers; very often that is not the case.

16. Unwarranted linking of sense and reference

Reference or denotation is the indication of some nonlinguistic entity by means of a linguistic symbol (for our purposes, a word). Not all words are referential. Proper names clearly are: "Moses" denotes or refers to a certain historical man with that name; "grace" in many Pauline contexts is at least partially referential, in that it refers to or denotes an attribute of God. However, the sense or meaning of a word is not its referent but the mental content with which that word is associated. Some words, notably abstract adjectives, have meaning but no referent (e.g., "beautiful").[87]

Clearly, then, sense and reference can be distinguished. But probably the majority of biblical scholars use these categories with less precision than linguists do. For instance, an expositor may say that such and such a word denotes X—where X is not the referent but the sense of the word.[88]

But the reason these considerations are important for our purposes is that many of the word-study fallacies considered in this chapter presuppose a reference view of meaning—that is, words in this view are thought to be related to reality by naming real entities. This encourages the faulty notion that a word has a "basic meaning." Perhaps the best refutation of this view is that of Gilbert Ryle, who compares two sets of five words:

a. three is a prime number
b. Plato, Aristotle, Aquinas, Locke, Berkeley[89]

87. For further discussion, see Silva, *Biblical Words and Their Meaning*, 101–18; and especially Gibson, *Biblical Semantic Logic*, 47–59. The two authors use their terms in slightly different ways. Gibson uses "meaning" approximately the way Silva uses "sense."
88. There are many examples in Thomas E. McComiskey, "Exegetical Notes: Micah 7," *Trinity Journal* 2 (1981): 62–68.
89. Gilbert Ryle, "The Theory of Meaning," in *Philosophy and Ordinary Language*, ed. Charles E. Caton (Urbana, Ill.: University of Illinois, 1963), 133.

Now if every word were a name, then each of the five words in the two sets would have to refer to an extralinguistic reality. This is true for b, but it misses the point of a, which, unlike b, is a sentence. A sentence cannot be analyzed into the things each word in the sentence "names." It follows that the meaning of words in a grammatically coherent array, as in a, is different from the theoretical referent of each word.

Failure to understand these matters was one of the forces that led to the *Theological Dictionary of the New Testament*, especially the early volumes. The very nature of the presentation argues implicitly (and sometimes explicitly) that words primarily refer to extralinguistic realities, so that not only can the realities be understood by word studies, but the words themselves take on immense freight. But as important as word studies are, it is very doubtful if profound understanding of any text or of any theme is really possible by word studies alone.

The Heart of the Matter: Coping with Context

Perhaps the principal reason why word studies constitute a particularly rich source for exegetical fallacies is that many preachers and Bible teachers know Greek only well enough to use concordances, or perhaps a little more. There is little feel for Greek as a language; and so there is the temptation to display what has been learned in study, which as often as not is a great deal of lexical information without the restraining influence of context. The solution, of course, is to learn more Greek, not less, and to gain at least a rudimentary knowledge of linguistics.

To go beyond the list this chapter has provided and try to provide some positive guidelines would be to transform the purpose of this book; so I refrain. But the heart of the issue is that semantics, meaning, is more than the meaning of words. It involves phrases, sentences, discourse, genre, style; it demands a feel for not only syntagmatic word studies (those that relate words to other words) but also paradigmatic word studies (those that ponder why *this* word is used instead of *that* word). I have barely broached questions of metaphor and said nothing about purposeful semantic ambiguity. Other writers handle such matters more ably than I could; so for my part I shall press on to a consideration of a new list of fallacies.

2

Grammatical Fallacies

One might expect a series on exegetical fallacies to include far more examples, and a greater diversity of examples, drawn from the grammatical arena than from word studies. After all, in complex syntactical units there is a greater number of variables than in single words, and therefore a greater number of things to go wrong. It is like comparing a stripped-down Chevy and a space shuttle: assuming reasonable equality in workmanship when the two machines were put together, the shuttle will suffer far more breakdowns and require much more maintenance than the Chevy. I have been thinking of developing a corollary to Murphy's Law, to the effect that in any system the law triumphs either in proportion to the number of components in the system or in exponential proportion to the number of components in the system.

Nevertheless, I am keeping this chapter briefer than the preceding one; and my examples will by and large be fairly easy ones. There are several reasons for this decision. First, word studies cast up as many fallacies as they do because most seminary-trained pastors have enough equipment to generate them, but do not have enough equipment to make some kinds of grammatical error. Many are the students who has looked up every instance of ἐκκλησία (ekklēsia) in the New Testament and drawn some questionable conclusions; but how many have looked up every instance of the genitive absolute in the New Testament, performed an inductive study, and drawn questionable conclusions? Until very recently, such a list could be compiled only by reading through the Greek New Testament and noting every instance; therefore hundreds of common constructions have never been subjected to the inductive scrutiny which words have undergone. Second, grammatical analysis has not been popular in the last few decades of biblical study. Far more time and energy have been devoted to lexical semantics than to grammar. The result is a broad assumption that many grammatical questions are closed, when in fact they are not. And third, some grammatical fallacies raise questions of such enormous complexity that they ought to be treated in separate monographs before being introduced at a semi-popular level. I shall shortly refer to one or two of these.

The Flexibility of New Testament Greek

Before we begin this survey of some elementary grammatical fallacies, it is important to remember that the principle of entropy operates in living languages as well as in physics. Languages "break down" with time: the syntax becomes less structured, the number of exceptions increases, the morphology is simplified, and so forth. The practical significance of this fact is that the relatively more structured grammar of the period of classical Greek cannot legitimately be applied holus-bolus to the Greek New Testament. The results of the great papyrological finds that alerted New Testament scholars to this truth were widely disseminated only at the end of the past century. That means technical commentaries on the New Testament Greek text written much before the end of the past century are unreliable on many grammatical points. J. Armitage Robinson in his great commentary on Ephesians,[1] for instance, tries to apply classical structures to the use of πᾶς (*pas*, all, every, whole) in that epistle and thus draws many conclusions that are demonstrably wrong. Distinctions in classical Greek may be observed only relatively more frequently than in Hellenistic Greek; but even so, grammarians who have been trained in the classics need reorientation to Hellenistic Greek if they are to avoid certain errors when they read the New Testament.

1. J. Armitage Robinson, *St. Paul's Epistle to the Ephesians* (London: Macmillan, 1903).

Fallacies Connected
with Various Tenses and Moods

It is not altogether clear that "tense" is a very accurate way of referring to the "Greek tenses." The word *tense* calls up notions of time: present tense, future tense, and so forth. But suppose a verb form is *morphologically* "present tense" while not in fact referring to present time but to past time: then shall we refer to such an example as "past present tense"? The possibilities for confusion are boundless. To aid in the clarity of the following discussion, I shall use "tense" only to refer to morphological form, with *no* implications whatsoever with respect to time.

The majority of contemporary students of Greek grammar argue that Greek tenses are time-related in the indicative and reflect *Aktionsart* ("kind of action") outside the indicative. I am not persuaded this is right. A rising number of Greek grammarians argue that the fundamental semantic force of the Greek tense is "aspect": it reflects the author's choice of how to present an action. The time of the action is not conveyed by the Greek tense (which virtually all sides concede is true outside the indicative anyway), nor the kind of action that took place, but by the author's conception of that action—for example, an author might think of a particular action as a "complete" action, even if it took a very long time, and choose to use the aorist tense.[2]

With these distinctions in mind, it is worth reviewing some recent discussion of particular tenses (remember: by this I mean "tense forms"). I shall begin with the "standard" categories that are commonly deployed in Greek grammars, point out the difficulties and fallacies, and move toward an aspectual approach.

---

2. Of the rising number of works that might be cited, see especially Stanley E. Porter, *Verbal Aspect in the Greek of the New Testament with Reference to Tense and Mood* (New York: Peter Lang, 1989); Buist Fanning, *Verbal Aspect in New Testament Greek* (Oxford: Clarendon Press, 1990); Kenneth L. McKay, *A New Syntax of the Verb in New Testament Greek: An Aspectual Approach* (New York: Peter Lang, 1994). These important books do not agree in every respect, but it is astonishing what measure of agreement has been reached by those who have studied this question closely.

1. The aorist tense

More than two decades ago, Frank Stagg wrote an article about "The Abused Aorist."[3] The problem as he saw it was that competent scholars were deducing from the presence of an aorist verb that the action in question was "once for all" or "completed." The problem arises in part because the aorist is often described as the punctiliar tense. Careful grammarians, of course, operating within the traditional categories, understood and explained that this does not mean the aorist could be used only for point actions. The aorist, after all, is well-named: it is a-orist, without a place, undefined. It simply refers to the action itself without specifying whether the action is unique, repeated, ingressive, instantaneous, past, or accomplished. The best grammarians understood this well, and used the term *punctiliar* much the way a mathematician uses the term *point* in geometry—to refer to a location without magnitude. But just as the mathematical notion is not intuitively obvious, so also has the notion of punctiliar action been a stumbling block to many interpreters. Stagg provided many examples of grammarians and commentators who insist, for instance, that the phrase *all sinned* (ἥμαρτον [*hēmarton*]) in Romans 5:12 must indicate a once-for-all action, presumably when Adam sinned; that the presentation of the body in Romans 12:1 is a once-for-all commitment; that the repentance noted in Revelation 3:19 must be once-for-all action because the verbal form is μετανόησον (*metanoēson*); that the aorist ἐτύθη (*etuthē*) in 1 Corinthians 5:7 ("for Christ our passover lamb *was sacrificed*") means that Christ's death is a completed, once-for-all event; and so forth. And if grammarians and commentators draw such conclusions, who can blame the busy pastor for trading on the aorist to gain theological capital?

Stagg proceeded to give numerous counterexamples, a few of which I now pass on:

> "so then, my loved ones, as you have always obeyed" (ὑπηκούσατε [*hypekousate*], Phil. 2:12)—clearly not a once-for-all action or a temporally punctiliar action
> "but you, whenever you pray, go into (ἐισελθε [*eiselthe*]) your room" (Matt. 6:6)—again, repetition is presupposed

3. Frank Stagg, "The Abused Aorist," *JBL* 91 (1972): 222–31.

"what you have heard (ἠκούσατε [*ēkousate*]) from the beginning" (1 John 2:24, NIV)—clear extension over time "five times I received (ἔλαβον [*elabon*]) the thirty-nine lashes" (2 Cor. 11:24)

"they lived (ἔζησαν [*edzēsan*]) and reigned (ἐβασίλευσαν [*ebasileusan*]) a thousand years" (Rev. 20:4) "these all died (ἀπέθανον [*apethanon*]) in faith" (Heb. 11:13)—but clearly not all at the same time!

"transgressions and sins, in which you used to walk (περιεπατήσατε [*periepatēsate*]) when you followed the ways of the world" (Eph. 2:1–2)

"guard yourselves (φυλάξατε [*phylaxate*]) from idols" (1 John 5:21)—which clearly does not mean that if we have guarded ourselves once, the danger is over

"that he might show (ἐνδείξηται [*endeixētai*]) in the coming ages the incomparable riches of his grace" (Eph. 2:7)— which clearly does not mean God will display his grace just once in all eternity and get it over with

Even in the indicative, where the aorist usually refers to some action in past time, the pastness of the time cannot be counted on:

"in you I am well pleased" (εὐδόξησα [*eudoxēsa*], Mark 1:11) "the grass withers" (ἐξηράνθη [*exēranthē*], 1 Peter 1:24, NIV)

Stagg recognized, of course, that the presence of an aorist verb does not mean the action is *not* once-for-all or located in past time or temporally punctiliar. When we read that Sapphira fell (ἔπεσεν [*epesen*]) at Peter's feet, the context makes it clear that her falling was as "instantaneous" an action as that kind can ever be. Similarly, there may be contextual reasons for thinking that all persons did in fact die when Adam committed his first sin (see Rom. 5:12); it is just that the aorist verb ἥμαρτον (*hēmarton*) does not prove it. No believer doubts that Christ was sacrificed once only (1 Cor. 5:7), since after all some passages explicitly affirm this (e.g., Heb. 10:12); but this theological conclusion, as important as it is, derives no sure support from the presence of an aorist verb.

Stagg has not been the only one to warn against the abuse of the aorist;[4] yet one still finds not only preachers but also competent scholars making the mistake of resting too much weight on it. For instance, in the excellent commentary on the Epistle to the Hebrews by Philip Edgcumbe Hughes, we are told, regarding the opening verses, "The aorist tense, used both of God's speaking by the prophets (λαλήσας [*lalēsas*]) and also of his speaking by Christ (ἐλάλησεν [*elalēsen*]), indicates that God has finished speaking in both cases."[5] The conclusion, arguably, is theologically correct; but it is not proved by this argument. Commenting on 1:4, with respect to the Son's "becoming" superior to the angels, Hughes writes, "The aorist participle γενόμενος [*genomenos*], 'having become,' refers, as Spicq points out, to 'a dated event of history.'"[6] A final example comes from a recent article in which Heikki Räisänen, commenting on Romans 3:27 ("Where, then, is boasting? It is *excluded*"; NIV, italics added), writes, "In any case, the aorist (ἐξεκλείσθη [*exekleisthē*]) certainly means that the exclusion was a once-for-all act."[7]

Nevertheless, it is possible to go too far with this sort of criticism—a point well illustrated in a recent article by Charles R. Smith.[8] Smith draws attention to Stagg's work; and then not only does he argue that Stagg has been ignored, but also he seeks to go beyond Stagg by insisting that the evidence demands we ban forever all such labels as global aorist, constative aorist, ingressive aorist, and the like. An aorist is an aorist, he insists, nothing more; it is the "tense" used when an author does not want to use some other tense with more specifying force.

But this is linguistically naive. Let us for the moment remain entirely within the traditional categories for understanding the

4. See also K. L. McKay, "Syntax in Exegesis," *TB* 23 (1972): 44–47.
5. Philip Edgcumbe Hughes, *A Commentary on the Epistle to the Hebrews* (Grand Rapids: Eerdmans, 1977), 37 n. 6.
6. Ibid., 50 n. 3.
7. Heikki Räisänen, "Das 'Gesetz des Glaubens' (Röm. 3:27) und das 'Gesetz des Geistes' (Röm. 8:2)," *NTS* 26 (1980): 101–17, especially 110: "Jedenfalls besagt der Aorist sicher, dass das Ausschliessen ein *einmaliger Akt* war" (emphasis his). For support, he cites William Sanday and Arthur C. Headlam, *A Critical and Exegetical Commentary on the Epistle to the Romans* (Edinburgh: T. and T. Clark, 1902), 95. I am indebted to Douglas J. Moo for this example.
8. Charles R. Smith, "Errant Aorist Interpreters," *Grace Theological Journal* 2 (1981): 205–26.

Greek verb. We cannot fail to note that Smith reaches his conclusions by listing biblical counterexamples to each kind of
labeled aorist the grammars mention; but all that such counterexamples prove is that not every aorist is used in such a way, not
that no aorist is used in such a way. It proves, in other words,
that the diversity of patterns pointed out by Stagg and others for-
bids us from arguing that an action must be a particular type
because it is referred to in the aorist tense. Remaining with traditional categories, consider the Greek present tense: it can be
used to portray durative action, past action, iterative action,
future action, and more; but morphologically it is still the
present tense, nothing more. What gives the present tense any
particular shade of meaning is the set of relations it enjoys with
the context. Just as the meaning of a word in any context is
established in part by the set of relations that word enters into
with its context, so also the meaning of a tense in any context is
established in part by the set of relations that tense enters into
with its context. As a word is not infinitely plastic, but brings a
certain broad semantic range with it before it is shaped by the
context, outside of which range the meaning of the word will
only rarely move (as when a word takes on new meanings), so a
tense is not infinitely plastic, but brings a certain broad semantic
range with it before it is shaped by the context, outside of which
range the meaning of the tense will only rarely move.

But the very reason why the aorist tense can, *in its relations
with specific contexts*, portray an immense range of kinds of
action, is precisely because it is more plastic than the other
tenses. It has a more poorly defined semantic shape than other
tenses. But if we remain with the traditional categories it is still
appropriate to speak of a constative aorist in Hebrews 11:13
("these all died") where the context, interacting with the aorist
verb, demands that the interpreter understand the action as
constative. To say that this label is inappropriate because the
specificity is demanded not by the aorist tense verb but exclusively by the context betrays a fundamental misapprehension
as to how language works: the context says little about the
"constativeness" of the action apart from the semantic impress
it makes on the aorist verb itself. Thus, it is as linguistically
responsible to talk about a constative aorist verb as it is to talk
about a futuristic present or about the narrow, metaphorical

semantic range of the noun *pits* in the sentence *this house is the pits*. The unmarked noun *pits* does not succeed in suggesting the meaning of "pits" in the sentence; and the context *this house is the* does not succeed in conveying disgust and rejection either. But the context and the noun, interacting with one another, result in a clear expression of disgust in which "pits" is semantically unambiguous to those familiar with the metaphor. Similarly, ἀπέθανον (*apethanon*, died) is not a constative aorist; and the phrase *these all* by itself says nothing about constativeness. But "these all ἀπέθανον (*apethanon*, died)," in the context of Hebrews 11 where it is clear that although the deaths occurred over a considerable spread of time they are being lumped together in a summary fashion, is a statement in which it is entirely appropriate to speak of ἀπέθανον (*apethanon*) as an example of a constative aorist. The only thing we must remember is that the label *constataive aorist* is not meant to convey the results of morphological information, or even of semantic information borne exclusively by the aorist tense verb itself, but of semantic information borne by the aorist tense verb *in its relationship with the rest of this particular context.* The element of truth in Smith's protests, of course, is that the aorist *as aorist*, whatever it means, cannot of itself be thought to take on certain values (inceptive, gnomic, or whatever): the point is made as soon as you put down an aorist form of any Greek verb on a piece of paper and ask what kind of aorist it is. The question is a nonstarter: it simply makes no sense, until one provides a broader context. On the other hand, useful distinctions can be made from context to context, provided the grammarian recognizes—and all too few do—that such distinctions are prompted by the interaction of the aorist form and the surrounding context.

Linguistically, this means we should distinguish between the "semantics" ("meaning") of the morphological form and the "pragmatics" (of the context). From the preceding discussion, it should be clear that failure to make this distinction contributes to two different fallacies. The more common one falsely holds that the aorist tense always bears a highly specific meaning (usually identifiable as one of its "pragmatic" uses). The evidence clearly refutes this fallacy. The second argues that the aorist tense *even in diverse contexts* cannot, *in interaction with that context*, bear any semantic weight beyond the unmarked semantic value of the aorist. What this means for the interpreter is that a statement like "Because this is an ingressive aorist it means . . ." is unwarranted; but given the right context a statement like "The context shows this is an ingressive aorist, that is, the verb should be rendered . . ." may be perfectly legitimate.

None of this directly answers the question what a tense actually means when it is stripped out of any context—for example, what the semantics of the aorist tense are. Increasingly, grammarians who are linguistically trained argue for some such meaning as the following: the aorist tense "grammaticalizes" (that is, it puts into morphological form, into grammar) the author's or speaker's conceptualization of an event as a complete[9] event. I know that sounds complicated. But the point of such a definition is that there is no one-to-one connection between the Greek tense-form and the *time* of the action, or between the Greek tense-form and the *kind* of action (as if a certain kind of action absolutely demands a specific tense), but between the Greek tense-form and the author's choice of how the action will be conceived. Temporal constraints are introduced by other factors in the sentence or discourse (as in, say, Hebrew, Chinese, and many other languages). I suspect that over the next few decades the categories of linguistic analysis, and especially the categories of aspect theory, will gradually work themselves into the standard grammars and commentaries on the Greek New Testament.

2. The first person aorist subjunctive

I would like to use this entry as a sample case—a sample of the kinds of questions that further grammatical study turns up.

Using GRAMCORD computer facilities,[10] one of my students, Paul Barger, called up every instance of the first person aorist subjunctive in the Greek New Testament. He began by dividing these into two groups, singular and plural. Then he attempted to analyze the results, testing his findings against the standard grammars and commentaries.

---

9. Not necessarily a "completed" event, of course, as that would reintroduce the category of time.
10. See the discussion about GRAMCORD at the end of this chapter.

The results of his study do not concern us here, since my purpose is to expose fallacies, not formulate new grammatical rules. But the study of this grammatical unit quickly reveals how much work needs to be done on many points of exegetical significance. We begin by asking, What is a deliberative subjunctive? When is a deliberative subjunctive used? The answer, typically, is that the deliberative subjunctive is a first person (sing. or pl.) use of the subjunctive in interrogative sentences that deal with what is necessary, desirable, possible, or doubtful. The need is for a decision about the proper course of action; sometimes the question is rhetorical and sometimes an answer is expected.

What I want to point out here is not exactly a fallacy, unless we can include under that rubric those grammatical labelings which are so inadequate they hide more than they reveal. The typical definition of a deliberative subjunctive (and there are several variations) actually covers three quite separate categories. The true deliberative, like the hortatory subjunctive, is intramural—that is, the first person(s) denoted by the subject of the verb pose(s) a question that must be answered by himself (themselves). The owner of the vineyard asks himself, "What shall I do?" (Luke 20:13); and the result of his deliberation is his own answer, expressed in his resolve to send his son. There are only seven examples of this true deliberative subjunctive in the New Testament.[11]

The second and third categories are both pseudodeliberations. The first person subject(s) of the subjunctive ask(s) the question not of himself (themselves)—which would make it a true deliberative subjunctive—but either of someone else, seeking a direct answer (a direct-question pseudodeliberative subjunctive), or else merely as a device to introduce a statement, with no hint of deliberation or of a search for an answer from an outsider (a rhetorical pseudodeliberative subjunctive).

"Should we pay or not pay?" the Pharisees and Herodians ask Jesus (Mark 12:14). The form is "deliberative" in the broadest sense: it is a question in the first person subjunctive (δῶμεν ἢ μὴ δῶμεν; [*dōmen ē mē dōmen*]). But of course, it is not a true

---

11. These seven can be further divided into two quite distinct subgroups, the volitive and the futuristic; but that fact does not concern us here.

deliberative at all,[12] since the whole point of the question is to force Jesus into making a statement. This is a direct-question pseudodeliberative subjunctive. Similar things could be said of Mark 6:24, where Salome asks τί αἰτήσωμαι; (*ti aitēsōmai*, What shall I ask for?"). The subjunctive, not the indicative, is used, because there is some uncertainty in her mind, some "deliberation" as to what the answer should be; but the example is nevertheless distinguishable from the true deliberative, since the subject confidently expects another party, in this case her mother Herodias, to furnish her with an answer.[13]

Similarly, when Paul in Romans 6:15 asks ἁμαρτήσωμεν ὅτι οὐκ ἐσμὲν ὑπὸ νόμον (*hamartēsōmen hoti ouk esmen hypo nomon*, "Shall we sin because we are not under law. . . ." [NIV]), the subjunctive is retained because the question is formally open-ended, deliberative. But it is certainly not a true deliberative, since Paul does not pose the question as a reflection of his uncertainty, of his thoughtful deliberation. Nor is this a direct-question pseudodeliberative, since he is not asking the Roman believers for their opinions. Rather, he is using a rhetorical device to draw his readers into his argument, a device that sets up the hearty μὴ γένοιτο (*mē genoito*, "By no means!" [NIV]). In other words, this is a rhetorical pseudodeliberative use of the subjunctive.

My point is fourfold: much grammatical territory remains to be won, the results can be exegetically useful, systematic distinctions must be worked out between semantics (of the morphological form) and pragmatics (of the context) and meanwhile not a few grammatical categories mask as much as they reveal.

3. The middle voice

The most common fallacy in connection with the middle voice is the supposition that virtually everywhere it occurs it is either reflexive or suggests that the subject acts of itself. Compe-

12. See, for instance, James A. Brooks and Carlton L. Winbery, *Syntax of New Testament Greek* (Washington, D.C.: University Press of America, 1978), 108; cf. A. T. Robertson, *A Grammar of the Greek New Testament in the Light of Historical Research* (Nashville: Broadman, 1934), 924, 940.

13. Contra James H. Moulton, *A Grammar of New Testament Greek*, 2 vols. (Edinburgh: T. and T. Clark, 1908), 1:185.

tent grammarians are not so naive, of course; but this fallacy has nevertheless found its way into many books and is usually introduced in order to shore up some favored doctrine.

In particular, several authors have strenuously argued that the middle verb παύσονται (*pausontai*) in 1 Corinthians 13:8 is exegetically highly significant.[14] Prophecies will be destroyed (καταργηθήσονται [*katargēthēsontai*]), knowledge will be destroyed (καταργηθήσεται [*katargēthēsetai*]); but tongues will cease (παύσονται [*pausontai*])—that is, there is no need for tongues to be destroyed (passive) by someone or something, for the middle (it is argued) suggests that tongues *will cease by themselves, because of something intrinsic to their very nature.* This interpretation of the middle is then sometimes linked with the view that tongues played a useful role in the church until the canon was complete (some take τὸ τέλειον [*to teleion*, "the perfect thing"] in v. 10 to refer to the canon); but from that point on, they are intrinsically obsolete and cease. The conclusion to be drawn is that there is no valid gift of tongues today.

Whatever the merits of this exegesis of 1 Corinthians 13:8–10 (and they are few), it is certainly wrong to rest so much on the middle verb παύσονται (*pausontai*). For a start, the middle voice has a wide range of implications. Sometimes it is deponent (e.g., ἔρχονται [*erchontai*]); sometimes it is used to indicate that the action is reflexive; that is, that the subject acts on himself, herself, itself (e.g., Matt. 26:46; 27:5; although this use is uncommon in the New Testament). Sometimes the middle is used when a subject acts for self (e.g., Mark 10:38, τί αἰτεῖσθε [*ti aiteisthe*]— "what you are asking [for yourselves]," NIV). Sometimes the middle voice suggests the subject *allows* something to be done (e.g., Luke 2:5, ἀπογράψασθαι σὺν Μαριάμ [*apograpsasthai syn Mariam*], "to be enrolled with Mary"). Occasionally a verb is active in some tenses and middle deponent in others (especially the future); and at other times the middle voice of a verb with an active voice has a semantic range set disjunctively over against that of the active voice. One never knows in advance; each middle voice verb must be examined in its own right.

14. For example, Stanley D. Toussaint, "First Corinthians Thirteen and the Tongues Question," *BS* 120 (1963): 311–16; Robert G. Gromacki, *The Modern Tongues Movement* (Philadelphia: Presbyterian and Reformed, 1967), 128–29.

When we examine the use of the verb παύω (*pauo*) in the New Testament, we discover that it regularly appears in middle form. In the active voice, its lexical meaning is "to stop, to cause to stop, to relieve"; in the middle, either "to stop oneself" (reflexive usage), or "to cease" (i.e., it becomes equivalent to a deponent with intransitive force). It never unambiguously bears the meaning "to cease of itself" (i.e., because of something intrinsic in the nature of the subject); and several passages rule out such overtones as the automatic semantic force of the middle voice form of this verb. For instance, in Luke 8:24, we read that Jesus rebuked the wind and the raging waters, and they "subsided" (NIV; ἐπαύσαντο [*epausanto*])—which clearly cannot mean that they ceased because of something intrinsic to their nature. Something similar can be said of the rioters who "stopped" (ἐπαύσαντο [*epausanto*]) beating Paul (Acts 21:32): they did so because they saw the soldiers, not because of some internal constraint (see also 1 Peter 4:1).

Fallacies Connected with Various Syntactical Units

1. Conditionals

Three fallacies deserve mention under this heading. The first is a common one. In first-class conditions, often called "real" conditions, it is often thought the protasis is assumed to be true; that is, the thing assumed is real. On this basis, many prefer to begin every first-class protasis with "since" instead of "if." For instance, in one commentary on 1 Corinthians, we are told, regarding 1 Corinthians 15:12–16: "The conditional sentences throughout this section begin with *ei de*, the condition being an assumed fact: 'If it is preached (as it is) that Christ has been raised . . .' (v. 12). The same is true of vv. 13, 14, 16, 17, and 19."[15]

This is in fact a fallacy. In a first-class condition the protasis is assumed true for the sake of the argument, but the thing actually assumed may or may not be true. To put it another way, there is stress on the reality of the assumption, but not on the reality of the content that is assumed. Thus, in Matthew 12:27, when Jesus asks, "Even if I cast out demons by Beelzebub, by

15. W. Harold Mare, 1 Corinthians, in the *Expositor's Bible Commentary*, ed. Frank E. Gaebelein (Grand Rapids: Zondervan, 1976), 10:283.

whom do your sons cast them out?" the assumption that Jesus casts out demons by Beelzebub is real, in order for the argument to work; but the thing assumed remains unreal, for Jesus did not in fact cast out demons by Beelzebub. Of course, in the example from 1 Corinthians 15:12–16, both the assumption and the thing assumed are in fact real; but that fact could not be established simply on the ground that the conditional structure to which this protasis belongs is first class.

Second, it is a fallacy to hold that third-class conditions (ἐάν [*ean*] plus the subjunctive in the protasis) have some built-in expectation of fulfillment, doubtful or otherwise. James L. Boyer has convincingly shown that the third-class condition simply indicates futurity without any implication about possible or impossible, likely or unlikely fulfillment.[16]

But third, Boyer himself falls foul of a fallacy when he argues that there is no clear "time reference" in the apodosis of third-class conditionals. After all, he argues, every apodosis is future in meaning, whether the verb is an aorist imperative, an οὐ μή (*ou mē*) subjunctive, with a present indicative, a future indicative, an aorist subjunctive with ἵνα (*hina*) or some other form.

In the earlier edition of this book, I argued that Boyer is right only if the time frame is established with reference to the speaker or writer: in that case, every apodosis of a third class conditional is future. But basing myself on the work of a former student, I argued that if the time frame is established not with reference to the speaker but with reference to the fulfillment of the protasis, then the tense of the verb in the apodosis becomes important to the question of temporal relations. Present indicative verbs in the apodosis indicate action coincident with the time in which the action of the protasis is fulfilled; future indicative verbs in the apodosis indicate action subsequent to the time in which the action of the protasis is fulfilled (similarly the apodosis with οὐ μή [*ou mē*] plus the subjunctive).

But all of this presupposes that the verb tenses are primarily time-based in the indicative. There are too many objections to allow that supposition to stand. Boyer is wrong to suggest that all the apodoses of third-class conditionals are future-referring;

---

16. James L. Boyer, "Third (and Fourth) Class Conditions," *Grace Theological Journal* 4 (1983): 164–75.

FIGURE 4

	Use 1	Use 2
Articular	(a) definite	(c) generic
Anarthous	(b) indefinite—i.e., qualitiative	(d) nongeneric (individual item)

I was wrong to suggest so easy an alignment with the verb tenses of the apodosis. For example, in Mark 3:24–25 Jesus says, "If a kingdom is divided against itself [third-class conditional], that kingdom cannot stand (οὐ δύναται [present tense] σταθῆναι [*ou dynatai stathēnai*]). If a house is divided against itself [third-class conditional], that house cannot stand (οὐ δυνήσεται [future tense] ἡ οἰκια σταθῆναι [*ou dynēsetai hē oikia stathē-nai*])." Clearly, "Jesus is not saying that whereas a divided kingdom is currently unable to stand a house will only fall in the future."[17] Two or three explanations of the change of tense in the verb δύναμαι (*dynamai*) are possible, but the temporal one won't work. Similarly in Matthew 18:13: "If he finds it [third-class conditional] he rejoices"—where the present tense in the apodosis clearly refers to action that is future with reference to the time of the protasis, not contemporaneous with it. Numerous other examples could be given.

2. The article: preliminary considerations

The definite article in Greek is extraordinarily difficult to classify exhaustively. I suspect that some uses are determined more by the "feel" of the speaker or writer of the language than by unambiguous principles. Nevertheless some guiding principles exist; and many errors are made by those who ignore them or fail to understand them. In particular, it is a fallacy to suppose that because the Greek text has an article, the English translation must have one, or because the Greek text is anarthrous at some point, the English translation must follow suit. Unlike English, Greek has no indefinite article; and its definite article often has functions widely different from the use in English of either the definite or the indefinite article. At the risk of oversimplification, we can schematize the fundamental uses of the Greek article as in figure 4. The chart is reasonably self-

17. Stanley E. Porter, *Verbal Aspect*, 318.

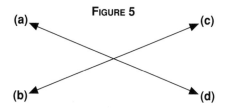

explanatory. One use of the definite article is to specify, to make a substantive definite. The corresponding anarthrous usage leaves the substantive *in*definite, not so much specifying it as leaving it "qualitative." The second general use of the article, however, is the generic (e.g., ἄξιος ὁ ἐργάτης τοῦ μισθοῦ αὐτοῦ [*axios ho ergatēs tou misthou autou*]) [Luke 10:7], lit. "the worker is worthy of his wages," but English idiom prefers "a worker is worthy of his wages"; the corresponding anarthrous usage suggests the substantive is *non*generic; that is, individualized (e.g., "*a* [certain] worker"). Many of the uses of the Greek article are subsets of one of these two general categories. For example, the anaphoric usage is a subset of (a); the preference of abstract nouns to retain the article can be considered a subset of (c).

What immediately stands out from this table is that there is a surprising conceptual crossover, schematized in figure 5. That is, the articular usage under use 1 has certain conceptual affinities with the anarthrous usage under use 2; and the anarthrous usage under use 1 has certain conceptual affinities with the articular usage under use 2. The very least that this means is that the exegete must be careful regarding conclusions drawn from the mere presence or absence of an article. Apart from certain idioms, only context and the feel gained by experience in the Greek text will serve as adequate control.

Grammarians, of course, understand these things; but it is surprising how many commentators do not seem to. For example, R. C. H. Lenski is notoriously unreliable in his treatment of the Greek article, frequently making appeal either to the presence (or absence) of the article in Greek to establish the corresponding pattern in English, or aligning the articular noun with a specific meaning (e.g., articular νόμος [*nomos*] represents

Mosaic law; anarthrous νόμος [*nomos*] represents the principle of law).[18]

3. The article: the Granville Sharp rule

Some grammars present the rule in a rather simplistic form, such as the following:

> Sharp's rule states: if two substantives are connected by καί and both have the article, they refer to different persons or things . . . ; if the first has an article and the second does not, the second refers to the same person or thing as the first. . . . Of course the rule could also be applied to a series of three or more.[19]

The initial fallacy is in formulating the Granville Sharp rule with less care than Granville Sharp did. Sharp's rule is in fact quite complex, too complex to analyze here. What is quite clear, however, is that he excluded plural nouns from his rule (not to mention other restrictions). Thus if one article governs two plural substantives joined by καί (*kai*), there is no reason to think that the two substantives refer to the same thing, even though the article groups them together so that in certain respects they function as a single entity.[20]

Failure to recognize this point lies behind the insistence of some scholars that Matthew is anachronistic in his treatment of the Jewish leaders. In Matthew 16:1, 6 and elsewhere, Matthew lumps Pharisees and Sadducees together under one article. Only those so far removed from Jesus' day (it is said) that they were unaware that Pharisees and Sadducees were separate and distinct parties could have used such a construction here. The fallacy, of course, lies in relying upon the Granville Sharp rule where Sharp himself explicitly insists his rule does not operate. The error of the commentators is at least understandable, since so many of the standard grammars also get this

---

18. For example, see his treatment of νόμος *(nomos)* in Galatians, in R. C. H. Lenski, *The Interpretation of St. Paul's Epistles to the Galatians, to the Ephesians and to the Philippians* (Minneapolis: Augsburg, 1937).

19. Brooks and Winbery, *Syntax of New Testament Greek*, 70.

20. Refer to A. T. Robertson, *Grammar*, 787; Maximilian Zerwick, *Biblical Greek Illustrated by Examples* (Rome: Iura Editionis et Versionis Reservantur, 1963), sec. 184.

point wrong, but Sharp himself can scarcely be blamed.[21] As I have shown elsewhere, only one article governs both nouns in expressions like "the Epicureans and Stoics" (Acts 17:18).[22] Indeed, the only place where τῶν Φαρισαίων καὶ Σαδδουκαίων (*tōn Pharisaiōn kai Saddoukaiōn*) is found outside Matthew is in Acts 23:7; and in this context the doctrinal disparity between the two groups is presupposed. In each pair, the two nouns are linked together for the purpose at hand. In Acts 23:7, the purpose at hand is the dispute that broke out between them. In Matthew 16:1, the Pharisees and Sadducees are linked in their question to Jesus, presumably as they function together as representatives of the Sanhedrin. In 16:6, 11, 12 the use of the phrase τῶν Φαρισαίων καὶ Σαδδουχαίων (*tōn Pharisaiōn kai Saddoukaiōn*, of the Pharisees and Sadducees) does not mean the evangelist thought the teaching of the two groups was identical, but only that in certain respects their teaching was alike—in particular its antipathy toward Jesus and the revelation he was bringing.[23]

At the other end of the scale, καὶ ὁ νικῶν καὶ ὁ τηρῶν (*kai ho nikōn kai ho terōn*, Rev. 2:26) does not in context refer to two people, one who conquers and another who keeps God's word. Rather, it appears to be a slightly cumbersome idiom to invest this obedient conqueror with a weighty label. The point in this case is that even where the text does not have one article governing two substantives, but two articles, one for each substantive, it does not follow that the inverse of the Granville Sharp rule holds true, such that there *must* be two separate referents.

4. The article: the Colwell rule and related matters

It is now well known that in a clause like καὶ θεὸς ἦν ὁ λόγος (*kai theos ēn ho logos*, usually rendered "and the Word was God," John 1:1), the noun with the article is the subject, even though

---

21. See especially the third edition of his work, *Remarks on the Use of the Definite Article in the Greek Text of the New Testament, Containing many New Proofs of the Divinity of Christ, From Passages which are wrongly translated in the Common English Version* (London: Vernor and Hood, et al., 1803).
22. D. A. Carson, "The Jewish Leaders in Matthew's Gospel: A Reappraisal," *JETS* 25 (1982): 161–74.
23. Ibid., 168–69.

it is placed after the verb.[24] The more difficult question in such cases is whether any rule governs the anarthrous noun before the verb: how do we know whether it is definite or indefinite, "God" or "a god"?

In 1933 E. C. Colwell published an important article that addressed the matter.[25] He studied definite predicate nouns (their "definiteness" was determined by his own judgment) both before and after the verb, both with and without the article. He observed, among other things, that if a definite noun preceded a copulative verb, it was normally anarthrous; if it followed, it was articular. Applied to John 1:1, this rule means it is quite responsible to take θεός (*theos*) to mean the definite "God," not the indefinite "a god," since according to Colwell 87 percent of definite predicates before the verb in the Greek New Testament are anarthrous.

Colwell's work has been widely cited, but it has some methodological weaknesses:

> . . . while the [Colwell] canon may reflect a general tendency it is not absolute by any means; after all, it takes no account of relative clauses or proper nouns, and he has also omitted a considerable class of "qualitative" nouns like that in ὁ θεὸς ἀγάπη ἐστίν. Moreover, he is the first to admit the lack of objectivity in his method of counting: he professes to include only *definite* nouns among his anarthrous predicates, and the degree of definiteness is extremely difficult to assess.[26]

Beyond even these limitations, however, Colwell's rule can easily be abused. The fallacy in many popular appeals to Colwell is in thinking the part of his rule that pertains to John 1:1 is based on an examination of all anarthrous predicates that precede copulative verbs. If that were the case, his figure of 87 percent would be impressive. But in fact he only claims to have examined definite anarthrous nouns (as he determines "definite-

---

24. See the important treatment by Murray J. Harris, *Jesus as God: The New Testament Use of Theos in Reference to Jesus* (Grand Rapids: Baker Book House, 1992).
25. E. C. Colwell, "A Definite Rule for the Use of the Article in the Greek New Testament," *JBL* 52 (1933): 12–21.
26. Nigel Turner, *Syntax*, vol. 3 of James Hope Moulton, *A Grammar of New Testament Greek* (Edinburgh: T. and T. Clark, 1963), 184.

ness"). Recently one of my students, Ed Dewey, used our GRAM-
CORD facilities to retrieve every anarthrous noun (including
definite, indefinite, qualitative, and proper nouns, with a residue
of ambiguous entries) that precedes the copulative verbs γίνομαι
(*ginomai*) and εἰμί (*eimi*) in the Greek New Testament. He discovered that definite nouns and indefinite nouns make up an
approximately equal proportion of the entire list.

In other words, it is a fallacy to argue, on the basis of the fact
that a predicate noun preceding a copulative verb is anarthrous,
that it is highly likely to be definite. Statistically this is no more
likely than the conclusion it is *in*definite. Colwell's rule never
claims otherwise: it *begins* with the criterion of "definiteness"
and then develops its breakdown. As such, it is still valuable, and
certainly allows for the interpretation "and the Word was God"
in John 1:1, if other contextual indicators suggest it (and they
do). Moreover, McGaughy has developed a new rule that makes
the conclusion quite certain in this case.[27] But Colwell's rule
itself must not be abused.

5. Relationships of tenses

Exegetical and theological fallacies arise in this area when
conclusions are drawn without adequate attention being paid to
the relationships between clause and clause, established (usually) by the verbal forms. For instance, I. Howard Marshall
interprets Hebrews 3:6b ("And we are his house, if we hold on
to our courage and the hope of which we boast," NIV) and
Hebrews 3:14 ("We have come to share in Christ if we hold
firmly till the end the confidence we had at first," NIV) as if they
say exactly the same thing, that "membership of God's house-
hold is conditional upon perseverance."[28] In one sense, of
course, that is correct; but close attention to the tenses in their
context in Hebrews 3:14 reveals an extra ingredient in this verse.
We have become (γεγόναμεν [*gegonamen*])—past reference, I
would argue—partakers of Christ if we now, in the present, hold

27. See the excellent study by Lane C. McGaughy, *Toward a Descriptive
Analysis of Einai as a Linking Verb in New Testament Greek* (Missoula, Mont.:
Society of Biblical Literature, 1972), SBL Dissertation Series, no. 6 along with
the slightly corrective review by E. V. N. Goetchius, *JBL* 92 (1976): 147–49.
28. I. Howard Marshall, *Kept by the Power of God* (Minneapolis: Bethany,
1969), 140, 152.

firmly to the confidence we had at first. It follows from this verse that although perseverance is mandated, it is also the evidence of what has taken place in the past. Put another way, perseverance becomes one of the essential ingredients of what it means to be a Christian, of what a partaker of Christ is and does. If persevering shows we have (already) come to share in Christ, it can only be because sharing in Christ has perseverance for its inevitable fruit.

The Potential for Renewed Precision

Surprisingly little progress has been made in Greek grammar during the past few decades, partly reflecting declining standards in classical education, partly reflecting interest diverted elsewhere.[29] Of course, there are many exceptional scholars who contribute substantially to the discipline; but much work needs to be done.

This situation may change fairly rapidly with the advent of the GRAMCORD package to which I have already referred in this chapter. GRAMCORD stands for GRAMmatical conCOR-Dance. Conceived by James Boyer and developed by Paul Miller, GRAMCORD is a computer retrieval system consisting of a tagged text of the Greek New Testament and a software program of considerable sophistication that enables the user to retrieve any grammatical construction of any length and complexity provided it is morphologically and/or positionally defined. I am presently working on a reference book that will put together many of the results in a form useful to Bible translators and grammarians. This will mean that much of the donkey work of collecting data can be eliminated, replaced by pushing a few buttons or by a convenient reference volume; and this will leave more energy for the analysis of data.

For instance, I recently wrote a command set to get the computer to retrieve every instance of the genitive absolute, and analyzed the results. This is the first time, to my knowledge, that such a list has ever been compiled. It includes such breakdowns as when the noun precedes the participle, or the reverse; when

29. See, for instance, Lars Rydbeck, "What Happened to New Testament Greek Grammar after Albert Debrunner?" *NTS* 21 (1974–75): 424–27.

the pronoun precedes the participle, or the reverse; the tense of the participle; various compound or defective genitive absolutes; and so forth. Or again, another of my students, Sung Yang, retrieved and analyzed every instance in the Greek New Testament of a singular verb combined with a compound subject, and formulated some rules on the basis of the thoroughgoing induction made possible by this exhaustive retrieval of data. Results such as these will shortly be published elsewhere. It is no part of my purpose here to introduce new grammatical formulations. Nevertheless these technological developments will make thorough inductive analysis of Greek grammar more manageable in the future, and will therefore contribute to the reduction of errors and the exposure of grammatical fallacies.

3

Logical Fallacies

Why Are Fire Engines Red?

They have four wheels and eight men;
four plus eight is twelve;
twelve inches make a ruler;
a ruler is Queen Elizabeth;
Queen Elizabeth sails the seven seas;
the seven seas have fish;
the fish have fins;
the Finns hate the Russians;
the Russians are red;
fire engines are always rushin';
    so they're red.

I do not remember where I learned this little gem, but it raises in an extreme form the subject of logic. We see the argument is ridiculous; but why is it ridiculous? What is the nature of the breaches as we move from line to line, or even within one line? Why should we not accept this argument as a valid answer to the question, "Why are fire engines red?"

The Nature and Universality of Logic

Before attempting to list various logical fallacies that frequently crop up in exegetical work, I must say something about the nature of logic. At the risk of oversimplification, I will distinguish four senses in which the word *logic* is used: "logic" at the theoretical and symbolic level is a comprehensive term that refers to sets of axiomatic relationships, "an analysis and evalu-

ation of the ways of using evidence to derive correct conclusions";[1] "logic" in common speech at a nontechnical level is a
synonym for words such as "workable," "reasonable," and the
like—a logical plan may be a workable plan, an illogical step
may be a rash step; "logic" sometimes means a formal presentation of an argument: that is, people engage in "logical argument," whether or not there are fallacies in the steps they take;
"logic" in common speech may refer to a set of propositions or
even an outlook which may or may not be "logical" in the first
sense. For example, we sometimes speak of "Western logic" or
"Japanese logic" or "the logic of the marketplace" or "the logic
of ecology." In this fourth sense, one logic may compete with
another logic: the logic of communism and the logic of capital-
ism are in competition at various levels. As Arthur Gibson has
pointed out, W. F. Albright tried to associate the "proto-logical"
with an inability to control by ordinary human experience,
dream life, religious phenomena, the "empirico-logical" with
the Hebrew Bible, and "formal logic" with ways of thought
among the Greeks.[2]

Now I am here interested only in the first sense of logic; but
because confusion over these various uses of the term *logic*
bedevils a great deal of debate, I must draw out the importance
of the distinctions a little more sharply. An exchange of articles
between John V. Dahms and Norman L. Geisler betrays confusion on this point.[3] For instance, Dahms says at one point, "The
aesthetic sense adds nothing to the matter at hand. It only determines whether the ideas and the empirical data are really compatible when logic says they are not compatible."[4] Now if Dahms
here uses "logic" in the first sense, he has uttered nonsense. If
logic in the first sense shows that certain data are incompatible,

1. William J. Kilgore, *An Introductory Logic,* 2d ed. (New York: Holt, Rine-
hart and Winston, 1979), 7.
2. Arthur Gibson, *Biblical Semantic Logic: A Preliminary Analysis* (New
York: St. Martin, 1981), 225–31.
3. John V. Dahms, "How Reliable Is Logic?" *JETS* 21 (1978): 369–80; Norman L. Geisler, "'Avoid . . . Contradictions' (1 Timothy 6:20): A Reply to John
Dahms," *JETS* 22 (1979):55–65; John V. Dahms, "A Trinitarian Epistemology
Defended: A Rejoinder to Norman Geisler," *JETS* 22 (1979): 133–48; Norman L.
Geisler, "Avoid *All* Contradictions: A Surrejoinder to John Dahms," *JETS* 22
(1979):149–59.
4. Dahms, "A Trinitarian Epistemology Defended," 134.

all the aesthetic sense in the world cannot show they are in fact compatible. But if he here uses "logic" in the third sense, to refer to an argument that is structured by logical categories that may involve fallacies owing to improper steps, inconclusive evidence, or the like, then the data may be judged incompatible by "this logical argument" (i.e., by this form of structured argument) while still in fact being logical in the first sense. Aesthetics *may* help us suspect that the data are in fact logical (first sense) despite the fact that logic (third sense) says they are not. But Dahms confuses the two senses of "logic" repeatedly. I have argued elsewhere that Jack B. Rogers and Donald McKim make exactly the same error when they say that John Calvin pits faith against logic (first sense).[5] Calvin does nothing of the kind. Rather, he pits faith against a particular logical argument (third sense) that he shows to be in fact fallacious.

The point is that logic in the first sense is universal. It is not to be dismissed as the peculiar debatable theory of Aristotle. Rather, it is the set of relationships (nicely formulated by Aristotle and others) that must apply if any knowledge is possible and if any communication of propositional knowledge is possible. Even peoples who prefer to communicate in largely picture categories use logic in this sense; and a dialectical theologian either holds that his apparently contradictory beliefs are ultimately logically compatible or he is talking nonsense. That is why, for instance, a person who holds that Jesus is both God and man goes to considerable trouble to formulate this truth in ways that are not demonstrably *il*logical, even if the explanation of this God-man's nature is not exhaustive. The necessary substratum of all coherent knowledge and of all rational communication is simple logic in this first sense. The fundamental "laws" of logic, such as the law of noncontradiction and the law of the excluded middle, are universally true.

We are now in a better position to survey various logical fallacies. In the list I am providing, other fallacies may supplement the particular logical fallacy under discussion, but it is the logical fallacy that remains in focus in this list. Moreover, some of

5. D. A. Carson, "Unity and Diversity in the New Testament: The Possibility of Systematic Theology," in *Scripture and Truth*, ed. D. A. Carson and John D. Woodbridge (Grand Rapids: Zondervan, 1983), 80–81.

the entries reflect the same error in logic as some other entry, but because they are different applications of that error, I have sometimes introduced distinct labels.

A Select List of Logical Fallacies

1. *False disjunctions: an improper appeal to the law of the excluded middle*

We have already considered semantic disjunctions (chap. 1, entry 11); but false disjunctions—a false either/or requirement when complementarity might be acceptable—are extraordinarily common and potentially very destructive of fair-minded, evenhanded exegesis. For instance, in listing various methods of interpretation, John D. Grassmick begins by mentioning what he calls the allegorical method;[6] and as an illustration he refers to Leon Morris's view that the 144,000 in Revelation 7 are to be identified with the Christian church.[7] Grassmick goes on to list several other methods, and comes to his own preference, "the grammatical-historical-contextual approach to interpretation."[8] Quite apart from the suitability of labeling Morris's approach "allegorical," Grassmick leaves the impression that Morris's method and his own method are disjunctive. In fact, whether or not we accept Morris's interpretation, every step he takes to reach his conclusion could be subsumed under Grassmick's method. The number 144,000 might be judged intentionally symbolic in a book of apocalyptic literature in which (all sides agree) numbers often have symbolic force. And Morris might want to make a case that in Revelation 7 the twelve tribes each providing 12,000 people constitute a typological symbol that is hermeneutically no different from typological symbols that Grassmick himself would be happy with elsewhere. We may evaluate Morris's reasons for such a symbolism as adequate or inadequate; but Grassmick has certainly not been fair to Morris insofar as he has imposed an unjustifiable disjunction onto the methods he lists.

6. John D. Grassmick, *Principles and Practices of Greek Exegesis* (Dallas: Dallas Theological Seminary, 1974), 9.
7. Leon Morris, *The Revelation of St. John* (Grand Rapids: Eerdmans, 1969), 114.
8. Grassmick, *Principles and Practices of Greek Exegesis*, 11–13.

Consider the conclusion of H. J. Held, when he discovers that where Matthew follows Mark, Matthew's accounts of actual miracles are considerably shorter, whereas the theological reflections on the miracles are more fully preserved: "The miracles are not important for their own sakes, but by reason of the message they convey."[9] Notice the disjunctive form: "not this . . . but that." We may well ask if *any* of the Gospel writers was interested in miracles for their own sakes. If Matthew merely shifts the balance of emphasis, why phrase the shift disjunctively?

Of course, some formal disjunctions are merely stylistic devices not to be interpreted as real disjunctions. Hebrew poetry tends to exhibit these devices and the New Testament also has its share.[10] "I desire mercy and not sacrifice" (Hos. 6:6) is formally disjunctive; but it is in reality a shock device to make people think about the incompatibility of offering sacrifice on the one hand while mercilessly nurturing enmity, bitterness, and animosity on the other. Mercy is more important than sacrifice; but the prophet is not proposing the prompt abolition of the cult. Similarly, we may hope that some formal disjunctions offered by modern scholars are not meant to be taken as anything more than rhetorical devices; but frequently the context of their writings strips away that charitable hope.

More difficult to isolate—and for that reason more dangerous—is the assumed and unformulated disjunction. Consider for instance this passage from Zane C. Hodges:

> It is an interpretative mistake of the first magnitude to confuse the terms of discipleship with the offer of eternal life as a free gift. "And whoever desires, let him take the water of life freely" (Rev. 22:22), is clearly an unconditional benefaction. "If anyone comes to me and does not . . . he cannot be My disciple" clearly expresses a relationship which is fully conditional. Not to recognize this simple distinction is to invite confusion and error at the most fundamental level.[11]

9. G. Bornkamm, G. Barth, and H. J. Held, *Tradition and Interpretation in Matthew* (London: SCM, 1963), 210.

10. See, for example, Maximillian Zerwick, *Biblical Greek Illustrated by Examples* (Rome: Pontifical Biblical Institute, 1963), sec. 445.

11. Zane D. Hodges, *The Gospel under Siege: A Study on Faith and Works* (Dallas: Redención Viva, 1981), 37.

In fact, not only in this paragraph but also throughout the entire book Hodges has assumed that there is a disjunction between grace and demand. He never wrestles with the possibility (in my view, the dead certainty) that in spiritual matters grace and demand are not necessarily mutually incompatible: everything depends on their relations, purposes, functions. The result of this assumed disjunction in Hodge's thought is not only what is in my judgment a false thesis—that the Bible teaches a person may be eternally saved even though there is not a scrap of evidence for it in his or her life—but also an array of exegetical and historical judgments that are extremely problematic.

2. Failure to recognize distinctions

A fine example of this fallacy—the fallacy that argues that because *x* and *y* are alike in certain respects they are alike in all respects—occurs in a recent article by David C. Steinmetz:

> Women may be forbidden to preach, teach, and celebrate the eucharist only if it can be demonstrated from Scripture that in Christ there is indeed male and female (contra Paul) and that in the last days sons shall prophesy while daughters demurely keep silent (contra Peter). Women already belong to a royal priesthood. Otherwise they are not even members of the church.[12]

Steinmetz is an excellent historian and a telling writer; but as catchy as these lines are, they do not prove what he thinks they do. Of course the Bible teaches that in Christ there is no male and female (Gal. 3:28); but does the Bible mean that male and female are alike in every respect? Who is going to bear the babies? Or do I now get my turn? The context of Galatians 3:28 shows the concern in that passage is with justification. In their standing before God, male and female are as one: neither enjoys any special advantage, each is acquitted by grace through faith. But Paul wrote other passages (1 Cor. 14:33b–36; 1 Tim. 2:11–15) which, on the face of it, seem to impose some sort of distinctions between the roles of men and women in the church. Even if someone ultimately decides that those passages do not mean

12. David C. Steinmetz, "The Protestant Minister and the Teaching Office of the Church," *Theological Education* 19 (1983): 45–64, especially 57.

what they seem to mean, it is methodologically illicit to decide in advance that because male and female are alike in certain respects they are therefore alike in all respects.

The same is true, of course, of the other passages referred to by Steinmetz. According to Luke, Peter cites Joel to the effect that both male and female shall prophesy (Acts 2:17); and certainly in the New Testament women do in fact prophesy (Acts 21:9; 1 Cor. 11:2–16). But Peter also says that the woman is the weaker vessel (1 Pet. 3:7). Whether this is taken with respect to physical strength or something else, it entails some sort of distinction; and a very good case can be made from New Testament evidence that a distinction was drawn between the gift of prophecy, which men and women could equally enjoy, and the church-recognized teaching authority over men, which only men could discharge.[13] Similar things could be said regarding Steinmetz's treatment of "royal priesthood." However one comes out on what the Bible as a whole actually says regarding the role relationships of men and women, the argument presented by Steinmetz is an example of a frequently repeated fallacy.

3. Appeal to selective evidence

From another perspective, the example from Steinmetz's writings can be seen not only as a failure to recognize distinctions, but also as an instance where there has been so selective a use of evidence that other evidence has been illegitimately excluded. We noted this problem in connection with word studies (chap. 1, entry 10), but of course it has much broader application. As a general rule, the more complex and/or emotional the issue, the greater the tendency to select only part of the evidence, prematurely construct a grid, and so filter the rest of the evidence through the grid that it is robbed of any substance. What is needed is evenhandedness, along with a greater desire for fidelity than for originality in the interpretation of the

13. See especially James B. Hurley, *Man and Woman in Biblical Perspective* (Grand Rapids: Zondervan, 1981); Stephen B. Clark, *Man and Woman in Christ: An Examination of the Roles of Men and Women in Light of Scripture and the Social Sciences* (Ann Arbor: Servant, 1980); Wayne A. Grudem, *The Gift of Prophecy in 1 Corinthians* (Washington, D.C.: University Press of America, 1982).

Scriptures. I dare say that many of the fundamental disputes dividing Christians, such as the manner in which to integrate God's sovereignty and man's responsibility, could be substantially and happily ameliorated if Christian leaders were to improve in this area. (I am presupposing, of course, that we *want* to improve; and sometimes that is only wishful, not to say wistful, thinking.)

An easy example is the appeal made by some very conservative Christians to 1 Corinthians 14:33–36 to argue that women should always keep silence in the church. They should not pray out loud, offer testimonies, or speak under any condition. Admittedly those verses by themselves could be taken that way; but such an interpretation brings us into unavoidable conflict with what Paul says three chapters earlier, where he permits women under certain conditions to pray and prophesy in the church (1 Cor. 11:2–15). The appeal to 1 Corinthians 14:33–36 to maintain absolute silence therefore reduces to an argument based on selective handling of the evidence.

4. Improperly handled syllogisms

I could introduce many scores of examples at this point, all of which betray one fundamental error in argumentation. The fallacy lies in thinking that certain arguments are good, when a moment's reflection exposes them as worthless.

Trinity Journal once published an exchange centering on the interpretation of 1 Timothy 2:11–15.[14] When Douglas J. Moo responded to Philip B. Payne's criticism, he sought to clarify some of the difference of opinion between them by restating some of the arguments of his opponent in syllogistic fashion. We need pursue only one example here.

Payne suggests that because 1 Timothy 3:11 refers to female deacons, and two of the men chosen as deacons in Acts 6:1–6 speak publicly and baptize converts, "presumably these activities could be part of the role of women deacons." Of course,

---

14. Douglas J. Moo, "1 Timothy 2:11–15: Meaning and Significance," *Trinity Journal* 1 (1980): 62–83; Philip B. Payne, "Libertarian Women in Ephesus: A Response to Douglas J. Moo's Article, '1 Timothy 2:11–15: Meaning and Significance,'" *Trinity Journal* 1 (1981): 169–97; Douglas J. Moo, "The Interpretation of 1 Timothy 2:11–15: A Rejoinder," *Trinity Journal* 2 (1981): 198–222.

Payne does not set forth his suggestion as a syllogism. Nevertheless, the inference he draws could be recast as a syllogism:

> The seven men appointed in Acts 6:1–6 were deacons (the unstated premise).
> Some of the men mentioned in Acts 6:1–6 spoke publicly and baptized.
> Therefore all deacons, including women, could presumably speak publicly and baptize.

Even if we grant the exegetically debatable points (e.g., that the seven men in Acts 6:1–6 were deacons), the argument as here set forth is inadequate—whatever we conclude about the right or otherwise of women to speak publicly and baptize. It is inadequate because it illegitimately presupposes that in the minor premise the two men from the group of seven in Acts 6:1–6 speak publicly and baptize by virtue of their role as deacons. In the New Testament, arguably teaching is irretrievably bound up with the role of elder/pastor/bishop; it is far from clear that it is bound up with the role of deacon. That others than elders taught in various settings is certain; but the fact that some deacons did so is not itself warrant for supposing that any deacon was authorized to do so simply because he or she was a deacon.

Among the different kinds of errors in syllogisms that one finds, perhaps the most common can be illustrated by the kind of reasoning represented by the following:

> All true Christians learn to love their enemies.
> Mary Jo loves her enemies.
> Therefore Mary Jo is a Christian.

This is of course exactly like the well-known canard:

> All dogs are animals.
> A cat is an animal.
> Therefore a cat is a dog.

No one in his or her right mind would advance the latter syllogism, but serious people advance the one before it all the time. That syllogism could be adjusted to become valid if the major premise were to read, "All true Christians, and only true Christians, learn to love their enemies." At that point, if "Mary Jo loves her enemies," she must in fact be counted a Christian.[15] It will be useful to illustrate this point symbolically. If

A = true Christians
B = those who love their enemies
C = Mary Jo

then clearly to say that A is a subset of B, and C is a subset of B, does not allow one to infer that C is a subset of A. But if (in the adjusted form of the syllogism) A = B, that is, all true Christians and only true Christians love their enemies, then if C is a subset of B, then it is also true that C is a subset of A.

The practical bearing of such observations is immense. Consider, for example, the argument of John Sanders.[16] He is concerned to show that some people other than those who self-consciously believe in Jesus may be saved. He examines Romans 10:9–10, where Paul says that those who confess with their mouth and believe in their heart that "Jesus is Lord" will be saved. "For it is with your heart that you believe and are justified, and it is with your mouth that you confess and are saved." But Sanders makes a distinction: "It is clear from Romans 10:9 that whoever confesses Jesus as Lord and believes in his heart that God raised him from the dead will be saved. It is not clear that whoever does not fulfill these conditions is lost. Paul simply does not specify how much a person has to know to be saved."[17] The matter, he says, is one of logic. Paul's argument is "logically similar" to the conditional statement, "If it rains, then the sidewalk will get wet." If the protasis is true, the

15. This adjustment makes the syllogism *valid,* that is, the logic holds up. It does not necessarily make it true. For example, it might be that there are some people who are not true Christians who have learned to love their enemies, thus falsifying the major premise. I return to the distinction between validity and truth in a later example.
16. I have used this example in my forthcoming book, *The Gagging of God: Christianity Confronts Pluralism* (Grand Rapids: Zondervan Publishing House, 1995).
17. John Sanders, *No Other Name: An Investigation into the Destiny of the Unevangelized* (Grand Rapids: William B. Eerdmans Publishing Company, 1992), 67.

apodosis follows: if it rains, the sidewalk is wet, and if you believe, you are saved. But it does not follow that if you negate the protasis, the negated apodosis is true. If it does not rain, it does not necessarily follow that the sidewalk is not wet, for it might have been soaked some other way, such as, by a sprinkler system. Similarly, if you do not confess with your mouth that Jesus is Lord, and if you do not believe in your heart that God raised him from the dead, it does not necessarily follow that you are *not* saved.

In terms of syllogism, we might arrange things several ways to follow Sanders' point. For example:

If it rains, the sidewalk gets wet.
The sidewalk is wet.
Therefore it is raining.

Or, better:

If it rains, the sidewalk gets wet.
It has not rained.
Therefore the sidewalk is not wet.

The invalidity of the argument in both cases is palpable.[18] By analogy, Romans 10:9, in Sanders' argument, must not be used to support arguments like these:

Whoever confesses with his mouth and believes in his heart will be saved.
Mary Jo is saved.
Therefore Mary Jo has confessed with her mouth and believed in her heart.

Or, better:

Whoever confesses with his mouth and believes in his heart will be saved.

18. In the second formulation, of course, the fallacy is that if a proposition is true, it does not necessarily follow that its negative is true. I shall give more examples of this in the next section.

Mary Jo has neither confessed with her mouth nor believed in her heart.
Therefore Mary Jo will not be saved.

At first glance, the argument of John Sanders seems unassailable, but it isn't. To return to my A, B, C example, his syllogism holds only if A is not identical with B. But if there are good reasons for thinking that A = B, then his argument will not work. If *all* who confess with their mouths and believe in their hearts are saved, and *only* those who confess with their mouths and believe in their hearts are saved, then clearly if Mary Jo does *not* believe she is not saved. Sanders has to assume that A does not equal B to make his argument work—and that, of course, is to assume the very thing he sets out to prove. True, Romans 10:9–10 does not itself prove that A = B, but if it can be shown that Paul's argument in Romans insists on this very point (and I think it can), then Sanders' treatment of Romans 10:9–10 is at best misleading.[19]

I turn to another example, one in which the syllogism is valid, but nevertheless the conclusion is false, because at least one of the premises is untrue. Consider this argument in favor of radical religious pluralism, advanced by Hans Urs von Balthasar:

> But what a tremendous panorama of freedom opens up for us from the vantage point of Christ's unity! "All things are yours," world, life and death, present and future, if "you are Christ's," for "Christ is God's" (1 Cor. 3:21ff.). The whole door opens on a single pivot; the plurality of all the forms in the world and in history, including death and the future, is accessible to the Christian's thinking and acting, if indeed he surrenders himself with Christ to God.[20]

There is much more of this, and finally an impassioned plea for radical religious pluralism. But it would be schematizing his argument only a little to configure it this way:

19. The above is an adaptation of the excellent treatment by Ronald Nash, *Is Jesus the Only Savior?* (Grand Rapids: Zondervan Publishing House, 1994), 145.
20. Hans Urs von Balthasar, *Truth Is Symphonic: Aspects of Christian Pluralism* (San Francisco: Ignatius Press, 1987), 86–87.

Paul says, "All are yours," and "you are Christ's," and "Christ is God's."
"All" includes everything without exception.
Therefore all religions must belong to God.

Quite apart from the fact that von Balthasar confuses God's providential ownership from his saving ownership, the form of the argument is valid, but the second premise is untrue. Von Balthasar has completely misunderstood Paul's words, as they are found in the context of the end of 1 Corinthians 3. As I have dealt with that passage at length elsewhere, I shall not repeat the arguments here, as the purpose of this book is to expose fallacies, not in every instance to set out an appropriate alternative interpretation.[21]

Many other examples can be found. It has long been disputed where in John 3:11–21 the evangelist intends to end Jesus' words and begin his own. R. C. H. Lenski tries to resolve the problem by saying that at very least verses 16 and 17 must be included in Jesus' reported speech, since in both cases the verse is connected with what precedes by the word γάρ (*gar*, for).[22] We may analyze his argument syllogistically:

Connectives such as γάρ (*gar*) connect their immediate context to the preceding context.
John 3:16 opens with a γάρ (*gar*).
Therefore John 3:16 is connected with the preceding context.

Again, the argument is valid, but is insufficient to prove Lenski's point; for he must show not only that γάρ (*gar*) establishes a connection, but also that the requirements of that connection would not be met if the evangelist located them in his logical conclusion of Jesus' preceding words. I myself am uncertain where to close the quotation in English orthography; but I am quite certain Lenski has not resolved the problem.

21. Cf. D. A. Carson, *The Cross and Christian Ministry* (Grand Rapids: Baker Book House, 1993), chap. 3; and especially Gordon D. Fee, *The First Epistle to the Corinthians* (Grand Rapids: William B. Eerdmans Publishing Company, 1987), in loc.
22. R. C. H. Lenski, *The Interpretation of St. John's Gospel* (Minneapolis: Augsburg, 1943), 258.

Again, in a book to which I have already made reference, Zane C. Hodges argues that the "tense solution" to 1 John 3:6, 9 is invalid—that is, that we cannot legitimately escape the force of these verses by arguing that John is saying only that *continual* sin is impossible for the Christian.[23] Certainly the present tense *in itself* is no solution; but certain features in Hodges' presentation do not stand up. He argues, for instance, that most Christians would not want to apply the same appeal regarding the force of the present tense to John 14:6b: "No one *continually* comes to the Father except through me," as if occasionally someone might come another way. Of course, he is right: no one argues that John 14:6 should be taken that way. Nevertheless, in this part of his argument he is implicitly charging *his* opponents with the following argument, syllogistically presented:

Present indicative finite verbs always have durative force.
The verbs in 1 John 3:6, 9 are present indicative finite verbs.
Therefore the verbs in 1 John 3:6, 9 have durative force.

Now to counter that sort of inclusive argument, all you have to do is introduce one counterexample. That will destroy the major premise, and the syllogism loses its validity. Perhaps some inexperienced exegetes would set things up this way and thus enable a Hodges to destroy their argument; but the more sophisticated would say that the present tense sometimes has durative force, and argue that contextually it is best to hold that the verb has some such force here. (I myself think that is true, although I do not believe that fact alone is a sufficient explanation of the passage.) But in that case, Hodges' argument at this point reduces to another syllogism:

There are many examples where the present indicative finite verb does not have durative force.
The verbs in 1 John 3:6, 9 are present indicative finite verbs.
Therefore the verbs in 1 John 3:6, 9 do not have durative force.

This is clearly an invalid argument, because the major premise is not universal. Hodges would have to show that the present

23. Hodges, *The Gospel under Siege*, 59–60.

tense never has durative force for the rest of the syllogism to be valid. Of course, these are not Hodges' only arguments; but these arguments, at least, do not stand up to close scrutiny. The fallacy is not only logical, but also methodologically akin to the linguistic and syntactical errors committed by Charles R. Smith in his article on the aorist, to which I have already referred.[24]

What we are dealing with, in part, is the distinction between necessity and sufficiency. This question returns in many forms.[25] It has considerable bearing on the formulation of doctrinal statements. For instance, a doctrinal test such as "Jesus is the Christ come in the flesh" is both necessary and sufficient when combating proto-Gnosticism (see 1 John 2:22; 4:2); but elsewhere, although it may be necessary, it is not sufficient. Similarly, the christological confession *Jesus is Lord* (1 Cor. 12:3) may be both necessary and sufficient when the problem confronted is the multiplicity of gods and philosophies each claiming to be "lord"; but it will avail little in John's conflict with proto-Gnosticism, where it remains a necessary test but no longer a sufficient one. If such logical points are not observed, creedal statements can easily degenerate to mere sloganeering.

5. Negative inferences

As we have just seen, one form of improper syllogism is the negative inference, but this form is so common that it deserves separate notice and more lavish illustration. It does not necessarily follow that if a proposition is true, a negative inference from that proposition is also true. The negative inference may be true, but this cannot be assumed, and in any case is never

24. Charles R. Smith, "Errant Aorist Interpreters," *Grace Theological Journal* 2 (1981): 205–26. See also chap. 2, pp. 72–75.

25. It came in a particularly awkward form in a series of letters from an unknown brother in California who wrote to criticize an address I had given in which I repeatedly referred to "Jesus" instead of "the Lord Jesus Christ" or the like. The chap felt I was demeaning Christ. I responded that when I preach from the Gospels, by preference I refer to the Savior the way the evangelists do—by calling him "Jesus." When preaching from Paul, I try to reserve distinctively Pauline christological emphases; and so on for the other biblical corpora. He replied by citing Rom. 10:9 as if it were a *necessary* formula *every* time the Lord Jesus is referred to. By such reasoning, I could as easily appeal to Matt. 1:21 to justify my practice. Unfortunately, the letter writer was unable to understand this point.

true *because* it is a negative inference. This can easily be presented in syllogistic form. Consider two examples:

All orthodox Jews believe in Moses.
Mr. Smith is not an orthodox Jew.
Therefore Mr. Smith does not believe in Moses.

This clearly does not hold up, because the conclusion depends on a negative inference from the major premise. Mr. Smith may be an unorthodox Jew who believes in Moses; or he may be a Gentile who believes in Moses.

Try a second example:

All who have faith in Jesus are saved.
Mr. Jones does not have faith in Jesus.
Therefore Mr. Jones is not saved.

From the perspective of New Testament theology, the conclusion is true; but the syllogism is invalid. In other words, this is an improper way of reaching a true conclusion. If the major premise read *"Only* those who have faith in Jesus are saved" instead of *"All* who have faith in Jesus are saved," then of course the new syllogism would constitute a valid argument.

In 2 Corinthians 13:5 Paul writes: "Examine yourselves to see whether you are in the faith; test yourselves. Do you not realize that Christ Jesus is in you—unless, of course, you fail the test?" (NIV). Calvin understands Paul to be saying "that all are *reprobates*, who doubt whether they profess Christ and are a part of His body"[26]—an interpretation which, as C. K. Barrett observes, "can hardly be said to follow."[27] Calvin seems to be arguing as follows:

Those who have confidence Christ is in them are saved.
Some Corinthians and others doubt (i.e., they do not have this confidence).

26. John Calvin, *Commentary on the Epistles of Paul the Apostle to the Corinthians*, trans. John Pringle, 2 vols. (Grand Rapids: Eerdmans, 1948), 2:397.
27. C. K. Barrett, *The Second Epistle to the Corinthians* (London: Black, 1973), 338.

Therefore those Corinthians and others are reprobates.

Now I do not believe that the major premise rightly interprets the text in any case; but even if we grant that it represents what Paul is saying, the conclusion does not follow because it is a negative inference. It reflects the Reformer's position that saving faith entails assurance of salvation; but it is not obvious that Paul is trying to make that point.

6. World-view confusion

The fallacy in this case lies in thinking that one's own experience and interpretation of reality are the proper framework for interpreting the biblical text, whereas in fact there may be such deep differences once we probe beyond the superficial level that we find quite different categories are being used, and the law of the excluded middle applies. James W. Sire offers several examples, for instance, of those steeped in the religious mysticism of the East thoroughly misunderstanding and therefore misrepresenting what some biblical text has to say.[28] Swami Satchitananda interprets "Blessed are the pure in heart: for they shall see God" (Matt. 5:8, KJV) to mean "Blessed are those who purify their consciences, for they shall see themselves as God." Quite apart from the unjustified introduction of reflexives, Satchitananda has imported his pantheism into the text, so that not only is the God of the Bible to that extent depersonalized, but also the ontological distinction between God and man is obliterated.[29]

This may be an extreme case; but there are many times we evangelicals take steps methodologically indistinguishable from this. We hear the Word of God commanding us to take up our cross and follow the Lord Jesus Christ, and so read our experience into the text that our "cross" becomes rheumatism, shortage of money, an irascible relative, an awkward roommate, a personal defeat, or even (God forgive us!) a joke. But we are far

---

28. James W. Sire, *Scripture Twisting: Twenty Ways the Cults Misread the Bible* (Downers Grove, Ill.: Inter-Varsity, 1980), 28–30, 128–30.

29. I purposely use the term *distinction* here rather than "disjunction," as the latter might be taken by some to rule out the *imago Dei*, or to overlook such texts as 2 Peter 1:4.

too light on ourselves; to the first-century reader, the person who literally took up his cross not only was condemned to die, but also was condemned to die the painful, ignominious, humiliating death Rome reserved for noncitizen criminals, the scum of the earth. If Jesus is telling us to take up our cross and follow him, the "death to self" he envisages is not death, nor some quick step of faith that kills off some ontological part called "the old man," but a painful, humiliating death made endurable only because Jesus physically passed this way first.

The fallacy at hand offers the clearest need for distanciation on the part of the interpreter (a notion explained in the introduction of this book). Unless we recognize the "distance" that separates us from the text being studied, we will overlook differences of outlook, vocabulary, interest; and quite unwittingly we will read our mental baggage into the text without pausing to ask if that is appropriate. We are truly prepared to understand a text only after we have understood some of the differences between what the text is talking about and what we gravitate to on the same subject. Failure to recognize the nature and scope of our own mental equipment is to commit what David Hackett Fischer calls the Baconian fallacy:

> The *Baconian fallacy* consists in the idea that a historian can operate without the aid of preconceived questions, hypotheses, ideas, assumptions, theories, paradigms, postulates, prejudices, presumptions, or general presuppositions of any kind. He is supposed to go a-wandering through the dark forest of the past, gathering facts like nuts and berries, until he has enough to make a general truth. Then he is to store up his general truths until he has the whole truth. This idea is double deficient, for it commits a historian to the pursuit of an impossible object by an impracticable method.[30]

This does not mean real knowledge is impossible. Rather, it means that real knowledge is close to impossible if we fail to recognize our own assumptions, questions, interests, and biases; but if we recognize them and, in dialogue with the text, seek to make allowances for them, we will be better able to

---

30. David Hackett Fischer, *Historians' Fallacies: Toward a Logic of Historical Thought* (New York: Harper and Row, 1970), 4.

avoid confusing our own world-views with those of the biblical writers.

7. Fallacies of question-framing

This is a subset of the preceding fallacy. The old chestnut "When did you stop beating your wife?" still evokes grins, because it foists an uncomfortable situation on the person to whom the question is addressed. If he has never started beating his wife, a question about when he stopped is irrelevant. The questioner has imposed his or her understanding of the situation on the person being questioned.

Fischer gives a number of choice examples in the arena of historical study: "Why was American slavery the most awful the world has ever known?" (a question that asks why without first demonstrating the presupposed what); or again, "Was Reconstruction shamefully harsh or surprisingly lenient?" (a question cast as a disjunction of two components, even though Reconstruction may have been partly harsh, partly lenient, and partly something else).[31]

In Fischer's words:

> The *law of the excluded middle* may demand instant obedience in formal logic, but in history it is as intricate in its applications as the internal revenue code. Dichotomy is used incorrectly when a question is constructed so that it demands a choice between two answers which are in fact not exclusive or not exhaustive. But it is often used by historians in this improper way.[32]

But before we theologians smugly thank God that we are not primarily historians, we need to recognize that we ourselves tumble into many fallacies because of the way we frame questions. Perhaps we do not write books with titles like *Napoleon III—Man of Destiny: Enlightened Statesman or Proto-Fascist?* But we do manage titles like *Paul: Libertine or Legalist?*[33] How many evangelical theologians (especially in North America) expend large amounts of energy asking whether 1 Thessalonians 4:13–18 teaches or presupposes a pretribulation or a post-tribu-

31. Ibid., 8–9.
32. Ibid., 10.
33. John W. Drane, *Paul: Libertine or Legalist?* (London: SPCK, 1975).

lation rapture, when on the face of it Paul's interest in writing that pericope is far removed from such questions? Or consider the (de)merits of disjunctive questions such as "Did Jesus die because of his spiritual agony or because of physical depletion?"

8. Unwarranted confusion of truth and precision

Occasionally the Scripture's truthfulness is depreciated because of its demonstrable imprecision. But it is a fallacy to confuse these two categories, or to think there is any entailment from the second to the first.

Wayne A. Grudem has recently treated this matter well.[34] As an illustration, he offers three sentences:

    a. My home is not far from my office.
    b. My home is about one and a half miles from my office.
    c. My home is 1.6 miles from my office.

Each of these three statements is true; but they are not equally precise. Many other examples could be given: the rounding off of integers, the use of phenomenological language to describe events in the physical world (e.g., the sun rises), the nature of reported speech. In none of these cases is there an entailment from the degree of precision or imprecision to the question of truth, unless the text gives the unmistakable impression that a higher degree of precision is being supplied than is in fact the case.

9. Purely emotive appeals

There is nothing intrinsically wrong with emotion, of course. Indeed, it is scarcely proper to preach and teach about heaven and hell, justification and condemnation, and the forgiveness and retention of sins without expressing any emotion whatsoever. But emotive appeals sometimes mask issues or hide the defectiveness of the underlying rational argument. An emotional appeal based on truth reflects sincerity and conviction; an emotional appeal used as a substitute for truth is worthless

34. Wayne A. Grudem, "Scripture's Self-Attestation and the Problem of Formulating a Doctrine of Scripture," in *Scripture and Truth*, ed. D. A. Carson and John D. Woodbridge (Grand Rapids: Zondervan, 1983), 51–53.

(although unfortunately often successful in winning the gullible). The fallacy lies in thinking that emotion can substitute for reason, or that it has logical force.

Sadly, the more disputed the issue, the more frequent will be the illegitimate emotional appeals; and sometimes these will be laced with sarcasm. "Calling and not sex is the test of authentic ministry," writes Steinmetz; "the church has been called to prove the spirits, not determine the gender."[35] The statement is cute, emotive, slightly sardonic—and worthless as a rational argument, unless the author has already shown that "proving the spirits" (1 John 4) has to do with determining general competence for ministry (it does not) and is set over against "determining the gender" (for otherwise the two might be complementary, not antithetical). But emotions are so high on this issue that the worthlessness of the argument will not be spotted by most readers until long after it has had significant psychological effect.

Sometimes a mild case of emotional abuse occurs when one writer responds to another with some such phrasing as this: "Astonishingly, Prof. Smith fails to take into account the fact that. . . ." Sometimes, of course, what Prof. Smith does or does not take into account is indeed astonishing. For example, if Prof. Smith claims to have provided a complete list of the uses of a word as found in the New Testament canon, but in fact leaves several important ones out, then of course the omission is astonishing. But if he does not claim to provide a complete list, to say that the omission is astonishing or surprising is a trifle manipulative.

I'm not sure if I have always been careful enough in this area; I shall try to do better in the future. But I have also been on the receiving end of this sort of dismissal. For instance, in an essay evaluating and at points gently critiquing the Vineyard Christian Movement, I pointed out that miracles sometimes have positive associations in the New Testament, and sometimes negative.[36] My esteemed colleague Wayne Grudem finds fault

---

35. David C. Steinmetz, "The Protestant Minister and the Teaching Office of the Church," *ATS Theological Education* 19 (1983): 57.

36. Cf. D. A. Carson, "The Purpose of Signs and Wonders in the New Testament," in *Power Religion: The Selling Out of the Evangelical Church,* ed. Michael Scott Horton (Chicago: Moody Press, 1992), 89–118.

with my list of examples: "Surprisingly, he [Carson] fails to discuss several of the positive passages mentioned above."[37] But surely this is tilted: I did not provide an exhaustive list of examples on the other side, either, nor did I give any indication that I was offering an exhaustive list of instances. "Surprisingly" in this case is merely an emotive appeal.

Appeal to emotional arguments can extend to the ways in which data are presented. Consider, for instance, the chart of the "Husband's Role in Headship Models" prepared by Lawrence O. Richards (see fig. 6). Even the hastiest reading shows how the material is skewed to drive the reader in the direction Richards wants; and the result is a biblical interpretation of the relevant passages that comes out (surprise! surprise!) just where Richards' "servant" model might expect it. But it would be just as fair to prepare a parody of Richards' chart (fig. 7), in order to drive readers in a somewhat different direction. My parody, as ridiculous as it is, is no less valid as an argument than the chart prepared by Richards. In fact, not to put too fine a point on it, most of Richards' exegesis in this connection is without real value, and much of it is wrong, because he constantly falls into fallacies of question framing, of world-view confusion, and of purely emotional and emotive appeals.[38]

10. Unwarranted generalization and overspecification

The fallacy in this case is in thinking that a particular can be extended to a generalization just because it suits what we want the text to say, or in thinking that a text says more than it actually says.

The false generalization is well exemplified in Walter J. Chantry's little book about *Today's Gospel*.[39] By and large I agree with its thesis that a great deal of modern evangelism is defective in that it fails to establish need before trying to present the full

37. Wayne Grudem, *Systematic Theology: An Introduction to Biblical Doctrine* (Grand Rapids: Zondervan Publishing House, 1994), 360 n. 12.

38. In the two charts, "ERA" stands for Equal Rights Amendment, which at the time of Richards' book and of my response was an issue of enormous symbolic import for many writers and speakers who were actively defending or attacking feminism.

39. Walter J. Chantry, *Today's Gospel: Authentic or Synthetic?* (Edinburgh: Banner of Truth, 1970).

FIGURE 6 HUSBAND'S ROLE IN HEADSHIP MODELS*

Command Model	Sharing Model	Servant Model

A husband who sees his headship in terms of this model will be likely to	A husband who sees headship in terms of this model will be likely to	A husband who sees headship in terms of this model will be likely to
make most significant decisions himself	make decision making a 50/50 matter	engage in consensus rather than authoritarian or compromise decision making
share few if any feelings	share himself and his feelings more fully	actively seek and try to understand his wife's thoughts, feelings, and needs
perceive headship in terms of authority and the right to require obedience	adopt compromise as the best way to resolve differences	encourage his wife to develop her full potential and use all her abilities
stereotype male and female roles in family and society	value intimacy over performance of "wife" role tasks	be more interested in personal growth and development than tasks and roles
make strict divisions between "women's work" and "men's work" around the home	consider his wife's feelings and ideas	place high priority on time with his wife and family
not want his wife to work outside the home	be unthreatened by the possibility of his wife working outside the home	
be strongly against ERA		

*From Lawrence O. Richards, *A Theology of Church Leadership*, 26. Copyright 1980 by Lawrence O. Richards. Used by permission of Zondervan Publishing House.

parameters of grace. But Chantry seeks to analyze the problem solely in terms of his exposition of Mark 10:17–27, the pericope about the rich young ruler. We are exhorted to "look closely at the Master Evangelist" and "note His methods."[40] That is good advice; but what Chantry fails to do is provide a rationale for his choice of *this* pericope. His argument almost requires that Jesus (and we) confront every sinner exactly the way Jesus deals with the rich young ruler. But one of the remarkable features about Jesus' earthly ministry is the amazing flexibility and adaptability of his approaches. There are often common ingredients, of course; but the fact remains that Jesus does not deal with Nicodemus exactly the way he handles the rich young ruler, and he does not respond to the Syro-Phoenician woman exactly as he did to the two men.

Another example crops up in the magisterial study by Stephen B. Clark. In attempting to refute Christian feminists who take Galatians 3:28 as a banner for the obliteration of role distinctions between men and women under Christ, he argues that the other pairs—slave/free, Jew/Gentile—are not abolished in Christ, so there is little reason to think the male/female pair is any different. In the case of Jew and Greek (Gentile), Clark points out that many early Jewish Christians did in fact continue to follow the Mosaic law, and adds: "In fact, Paul probably upheld the principle that if someone was circumcised, he should obey the Pentateuchal law (Gal. 5:3; 1 Cor. 7:18)."[41] Now arguably Clark can make a case for his general position; but this appeal to two verses from Paul to establish a broad attitude toward a large issue of eminent complexity smacks of unwarranted generalization from two texts. Indeed, it is not clear Clark has rightly understood the two verses he adduces. In the former, Galatians 5:3, Paul seems to be addressing the Christian Gentile who allows himself at that point in his life to be circumcised. The apostle is not here commenting on whether or not Jews circumcised at birth should or should not continue to follow all the stipulations of the Mosaic code after they have become Christians. And in the second, 1 Corinthians 7:18, Paul's point is surely that, as a general principle, becoming a Christian

40. Ibid., 17–18.
41. Clark, *Man and Woman in Christ*, 157.

FIGURE 7 HUSBAND'S ROLE IN HEADSHIP MODELS

Command Model	Sharing Model	Servant Model

A husband who sees headship in terms of this model will be likely to	A husband who sees headship in terms of this model will be likely to	A husband who sees headship in terms of this model will be likely to
responsibly grasp the strategic importance of providing leadership in decision-making	be unable to decide much on his own, but seek shared responsibility and blame	serve others in parasite fashion, drifting with *their* decisions
responsibly discipline his emotional life and understand the emotions of others	wear his emotions on his sleeve, and demand his wife do the same	display his emotions in emotional blackmail
perceive the biblical responsibilities in headship and seek to discharge his authority lovingly, knowing his wife can achieve her full potential only if he relieves her of burdens not rightly hers	adopt (frequently unbiblical) compromises as the best way to resolve differences	be hen-pecked, generally weak; destroy his wife's potential by forcing her to exercise leadership he has abdicated
preserve strong, traditional male/female roles in family and society	value "intimacy" or "sharing" over biblical responsibilities	be more interested in narcissistic personal development and approval of faddish friends than in obedience to God
listen to and consider his wife's ideas and feelings, soliciting all input that will contribute to the well-being of the family for which he is responsible to God	listen to and consider his wife's feelings and ideas, and end up indecisive	try so hard to respond to his wife's ideas and feelings that he provides no stability for her

(continued)

(Figure 7—continued)

Exegetical Fallacies

Command Model	Sharing Model	Servant Model
encourage full development of his wife's potential, without obliterating biblical boundaries between roles of men and women	so insist on sharing that he forces his wife to take a salaried job, even though the three children are still preschoolers	insist on being a house-husband
strongly oppose ERA where it poses dangers for Christian truth and obedience, while insisting equally strongly (because he is secure) on such principles of justice as equal pay for equal work	support ERA without mature, biblical reflection	gladly send his wife to the front lines of armed conflict while remaining at home himself in supporting roles

has no *necessary* bearing on whether an individual's station in life changes. A slave, for instance, should not think that his conversion to Christ entitles him to be free from his slavery (7:21a)—although Paul hastens to add, "If you can gain your freedom, do so" (7:21b, NIV). Paul can scarcely be telling the Jewish convert he *must* remain faithful to the law in all respects, when in the verse immediately succeeding the one cited by Clark he adds, "Circumcision is nothing and uncircumcision is nothing" (7:19, NIV)—which is not exactly what the law says! But even if Clark were right in his understanding of these two verses, he would still not have adequate grounds for his broader conclusions regarding the responsibility of Jewish Christians to keep the law; for he has generalized from just two verses, when many other passages that bear on the subject seem at face value to force modifications in his conclusions. To give one example, in 1 Corinthians 9:19–23 Paul is prepared to become like a Jew, keeping the law, or like a Gentile without the law, because he himself occupies a third ground, a distinctively Christian ground; and clearly he could not say such things if he felt bound, as a Christian Jew, to observe all the stipulations of Torah.[42]

Faulty generalization is also partly at stake in another exchange I have had over the subject of miracles. In the article

42. See D. A. Carson, "Pauline Inconsistency: Reflections on 1 Cor. 9:19–23 and Gal. 2:11–14," *Churchman* 100 (1986): 6–45.

to which I have already referred, I argued that the New Testament warnings about misleading miracles are substantial, and insufficiently taken into account by many Vineyard leaders. Jesus goes so far as to say that on the last day "many" will protest that they have cast out demons *in Jesus' name* and performed miracles in his name, but Jesus will banish them from his presence as "workers of iniquity" whom he has never known (Matt. 7:21–23). Indeed, elsewhere Jesus warns that great wonders will be performed by false Christs and false prophets, "to deceive even the elect, if that were possible" (Matt. 24:24). One interlocutor replied to the effect that the whole point of the latter passage is that the elect are *not* deceived: the clear implication, surely, is that "if it were possible" means precisely that it is not possible. Based not least on these considerations, he then argues at length that devout and honest Christians who humbly seek the Lord's will and blessing will not be led astray in such matters.

I think I could have been clearer in what exactly I was inferring from that text. I wholeheartedly agree that true believers will not *finally* be deceived. Yet that they can for a time be deceived by all kinds of things, miraculous and otherwise, is surely beyond dispute. For instance, according to Paul, Barnabas was deceived, at least for a time, by Peter's questionable conduct (Gal. 2:11–14). More importantly, there are many instances when people who are universally accepted as Christians in good standing are deceived, some so badly that there is every reason to wonder if, finally, they were really Christians at all. Ananias and Sapphira were deceived by the love of both money and a reputation for generosity, and consequently they lied against the Holy Spirit. Five of the seven letters to the churches in Revelation 2–3 warn about deception in the church, and suggest that if the members do not turn from the dangerous course ahead of them their church will be destroyed, while those members who prove discerning and faithful are the "conquerors" who are rewarded at the last day. Certainly Paul foresaw a time when vicious wolves would arise from within the Ephesian church, and warned the leaders of the church to prepare the people for that time (Acts 20). In his last letter to come down to us, Paul sadly confesses that "all those in Asia" have abandoned him (2 Tim. 1:15): doubtless this does not mean that *all* Christians there proved apostate, but it certainly means that there was enough deception operating to lead the believers away from Paul. More generally, it is hard not to see that huge swaths of the New Testament are written with the primary purpose of *un*deceiving Christian readers (think, for instance, of substantial parts of Galatians, Colossians, 1 Thessalonians, 2 Thessalonians, James, Jude, the Olivet Discourse, and so forth) or of warning them against false teaching or practices.

So my purpose in citing the few texts that I mentioned in the article to which my interlocutor takes exception is that Christians have been deceived and are often warned against being deceived. Moreover, for the purposes of that article it was important to say that the range of possible deception includes deception stirred up by miracles. It was not to argue from any one text or from the New Testament as a whole that any true Christian can be *finally* deceived and so lost. None of this did I lay out in detail, simply because I was writing a rather brief article.

But to argue from Matthew 24:24 that, because in that passage the elect are not deceived, therefore Christians who humbly seek the will of God will escape deception, is a curious interpretation. If the elect in the passage are not deceived *at all*, two things follow: (1) all the counterevidence in the New Testament is not easily explained; (2) it still remains the case, judging by the New Testament evidence I have briefly adduced, that many who are *thought* to be among the elect are eventually deceived, and thus prove reprobate—so a little godly fear seems to be in order. It seems much better, then, to take Matthew 24:24 to be saying that the elect are not *finally* deceived (the context is, after all, strongly eschatological), however much others may be, and, consonant with the way God's sovereignty frequently functions in the New Testament,[43] this is a call for believers to give extra attention to being discerning.

From my vantage, then, it appears to me that my interlocutor has taken a single text, rightly observed that the elect in that verse are not deceived, apparently inferred (wrongly) that this

43. E.g. just as election can be an incentive to evangelism (Acts 18:9–10), and God's work in the believer, even at the level of will and action, becomes an incentive to "work out" one's salvation (Phil. 2:12–13), so the assurance that the elect will not finally be deceived becomes an incentive to grow in discernment.

includes all deception, and generalized his conclusion in such a way that the bulk of the New Testament evidence is ignored. Overspecification is scarcely less common. Sire provides an interesting example in the Mormon treatment of Jeremiah 1:5, where God addresses Jeremiah in these terms: "Before I formed you in the womb I knew you, before you were born I set you apart; I appointed you as a prophet to the nations (NIV)."[44] Mormons appeal to this text to justify their view that Jeremiah actually existed as a "spirit child," as an "intelligence," before he was conceived. The words of Jeremiah 1:5 could just about be taken that way if there were contextual reasons for thinking that is what they mean, but such reasons are completely lacking. What the Mormons are really doing is appealing to their book *Pearl of Great Price* for the content of their doctrine, and appealing to the Bible at a verbally ambiguous point and overspecifying what the text says in order to claim the Bible's authority.

Unfortunately, evangelicals sometimes fall into the same trap. I have heard preachers argue, for instance, on the basis of the text "God will wipe every tear from their eyes" (Rev. 21:4, NIV) that at the judgment of believers there will be a great catharsis as our sins are exposed and then forever put away; but that is surely to overspecify the text, to read in a specific and limiting element not demonstrably present in the text itself. To hold to the Word of God involves us in the commitment not only to believe all that it says, but also to avoid going "beyond what is written" (1 Cor. 4:6, NIV).

11. *Unwarranted associative jumps*

This is a particular subset of the sixth fallacy in this chapter. It occurs when a word or phrase triggers off an associated idea, concept, or experience that bears no close relation to the text at hand, yet is used to interpret the text.

This error is shockingly easy to commit in textual preaching, overlooking the old adage that a text without a context becomes a pretext for a prooftext. An old favorite is Philippians 4:13: "I can do everything through him who gives me strength" (NIV). The "everything" cannot be completely unqualified (e.g., jump over the moon, integrate complex mathematical equations in

---

44. Sire, *Scripture Twisting*, 63.

my head, turn sand into gold), so it is commonly expounded as a text that promises Christ's strength to believers in all that they have to do or in all that God sets before them to do. That of course is a biblical thought; but as far as this verse is concerned it pays insufficient attention to the context. The "everything" in this context is contented living in the midst of food or hunger, plenty or want (Phil. 4:10–12). Whatever his circumstances, Paul can cope, with contentment, through Christ who gives him strength.

Or consider this statement: "The authority of the ordained minister is rooted in Jesus Christ, who has received it from the Father (Matt. 28:18), and who confers it by the Holy Spirit through the act of ordination."[45] The impression given is that Matthew 28:18 serves as biblical support for the entire proposition about the origins of the authority of the ordained minister. In fact, the chief connection with the text is the word *authority*, all of which the resurrected Christ claims has been given him. But the text says nothing about transmitting that authority, or some part of it, to a select subset of Christian disciples whom we label "ordained." Unfortunately, the document from which this example was taken is riddled with parallel uses of Scripture, making it hard to believe this item was an exceptional exegetical lapse.

12. False statements

It is astonishing how often a book or article gives false information; and if we rely on such a work too heavily, our exegesis will be badly skewed. Even ordinarily careful scholars make mistakes, sometimes because they have relied on unreliable secondary sources, sometimes because their own memories have played them tricks.

One little commentary on Hebrews, for instance, comments on Hebrews 3:1 ("fix your thoughts on Jesus, the *apostle* and high priest whom we confess"; NIV, italics added) by referring to John 20:21 as follows: "'As the Father hath sent (*apestalken*) Me, so send I (*apostellō*) you'; an *apostolos* is one who has been sent off on a mission by someone in authority, and so Jesus is the

45. *Baptism, Eucharist and Ministry* (Geneva: World Council of Churches, 1982), 22.

Father's Apostle, even as Christ sent His disciples off on His mission, making them thus His apostles."[46] The only problem is that the second verb in the sentence from John 20:21 is not ἀποστέλλω (*apostellō*) but πέμπω (*pempō*), making it unlikely that John was thinking of a commissioning of apostles. In any case, this is a plain error of fact, an unwitting contravention of the law of noncontradiction.

One well-known popularizer of Greek study is, I fear, prone to many of the exegetical fallacies catalogued in this book, not least this one. In defense of his interpretation of "I go a fishing" (John 21:3, KJV), which, he claims (on the basis of the verb and its present tense) means that Peter "is going back to his fishing business permanently," Wuest insists that his "translation and interpretation is based upon a rigid adherence to the rules of Greek grammar and the exact meaning of the Greek words involved." Perhaps he means to say only that this view is in line with his own "rigid" reading of Greek grammar. But he should have been alerted by the fact that *not one* of the major grammars or lexica supports his rendering; Wuest is supported only by a handful of old and relatively obscure commentators.[47]

13. The non sequitur

This refers to conclusions which "do not follow" from the evidence and arguments presented. There are many forms, often easily presented by the syllogisms I have already constructed several times in this chapter; but there are many examples that seem to be the result of muddled thinking or false premises that are not easily analyzed.

To begin with an easy example, Thomas H. Groome makes much of the truth that "the man without love has known nothing of God" (1 John 4:8) and concludes, "The only way truly to know God is through a loving relationship"—which does not follow.[48] But some of the worst examples I have seen come from

---

46. Gleason L. Archer, Jr., *The Epistle to the Hebrews* (Grand Rapids: Baker, 1957), 28.

47. The example is drawn from Kenneth S. Wuest, *Great Truths to Live By from the Greek New Testament* (Grand Rapids: William B. Eerdmans Publishing Company, 1952), 116.

48. Thomas H. Groome, *Christian Religious Education: Sharing Our Story and Vision* (San Francisco: Harper and Row, 1980), 143.

the documents of the World Council of Churches, doubtless because many such documents are written by committee and established by consensus. In one recent book, I note the following classic example of non sequitur: "Since ordination is essentially a setting apart with prayer for the gift of the Holy Spirit, the authority of the ordained ministry is not to be understood as the possession of the ordained person but as a gift for the continuing edification of the body in and for which the minister has been ordained."[49] There is in this statement a subtle shift from authority as possession to authority as gift for service, without proving that the two are disjunctive (can not one possess a gift for service?) or showing how the fact that the Holy Spirit is the donor has any bearing on the conclusion. Unfortunately, there are many statements similarly opaque in this document.

14. Cavalier dismissal

The fallacy in this instance lies in thinking that an opponent's argument has actually been handled when in fact it has merely been written off. To cite but one of many examples, Hans Conzelmann raises a possible interpretation of 1 Corinthians 11:4–6—only to banish it by adding the words, "This is fantastic."[50]

Often what is meant by such cavalier dismissal is that the opposing opinion emerges from a matrix of thought so different from a scholar's own that he finds it strange, weird, and unacceptable (unless he changes his entire framework). If so, something like that should be said, rather than resorting to the hasty dismissal which is simultaneously worthless as an argument and gratingly condescending.

15. Fallacies based on equivocal argumentation

By this general heading I am referring to arguments that cannot be written off as wrong, but that are nevertheless faulty, equivocal, unsatisfying. They claim to deliver more than they can.

There are many kinds of such equivocal argumentation. An interpreter may ask the rhetorical question, "Would Paul have

49. *Baptism, Eucharist and Ministry,* 22.
50. Hans Conzelmann, *First Corinthians,* ed. George W. MacRae, trans. James W. Leitch (Philadelphia: Fortress, 1975), 186 n. 42.

understood the law in such-and-such a way?"—meaning, of course, that he would not, so the option may be dismissed. Such a priori appeals have no logical force. How else are we going to establish what Paul means by law in the passage concerned than by careful exegesis?

More frequently, however, the rhetorical question I used as an illustration is not entirely illegitimate. It may be based on the unstated presupposition that the author has, in advance, concluded to his own satisfaction that law in Paul never means such-and-such elsewhere in his writings, and therefore it is unlikely to have that force in the remaining text, the one under discussion. If that is what the rhetorical question means, the argument may be unsatisfying because of its form but it does have some weight. But it is a fallacy to think this argument is conclusive, for there may be other relevant factors. For instance, Paul may be using the word *law* in an anomalous fashion, perhaps because he is dealing with a peculiar topic not treated by him elsewhere. My purpose in drawing these distinctions is to point out that even when an argument is valid, it may not be conclusive. Some arguments are intrinsically weak.

Less commendable is that form of argumentation that earnestly seeks out the most ambiguous language possible in order to secure the widest possible agreement. Such statements are worthless, because they paper over honest differences. They mask more than they reveal; and they verge on the dishonest or disreputable, for they coerce apparent agreement where there is no real agreement. Of course, it may be wise to skirt issue A by using ambiguous language if the purpose of the exercise is to discuss issue B, and issue A is nothing more than a red herring. But it is not a virtue to use the same language when discussing the real topic, issue B.

It is a fallacy to think that the following statements published by the WCC reflect any substantial agreement: "The members of Christ's body are to struggle with the oppressed towards that freedom and dignity promised with the coming of the Kingdom. This mission needs to be carried out in varying political, social and cultural contexts."[51] With a little effort,

---

51. *Baptism, Eucharist and Ministry,* 22.

Harold O. J. Brown and José Miranda could both agree to that statement! Or again:

> The Spirit keeps the Church in the apostolic tradition until the fulfilment of history in the Kingdom of God. Apostolic tradition in the Church means continuity in the permanent characteristics of the Church of the apostles: witness to the apostolic faith, proclamation and fresh interpretation of the Gospel, celebration of baptism and the eucharist, the transmission of ministerial responsibilities, communion in prayer, love, joy and suffering, service to the sick and needy, unity among the local churches and sharing the gifts which the Lord has given to each.[52]

It is difficult to see why either a Brethren assembly or the conservative wing of the Roman Catholic Church would have much trouble agreeing with that. Unfortunately, they would not be agreeing with each other: Almost every clause, sometimes every phrase, would be understood differently by the two traditions.

Another kind of equivocal argumentation occurs when a commentator wittingly or unwittingly phrases his presentation in such a way as to leave two or more options open—perhaps because he or she does not know the answer, or prefers to leave the matter masked or unresolved, or because there is an unwitting adoption of mutually incompatible views. For instance, Galatians 3:12, where the apostle cites Leviticus 18:5, is one of the major *cruces interpretum* of Paul's epistle to the Galatians. The question turns in part on whether Paul thinks the Mosaic law was ever capable of granting spiritual life or not. F. F. Bruce comments:

> True, in the context of Lev. 18:5 the promise of life to those who do what God commands is a genuine promise, but . . . in Gal. 3:12 Paul indicates that, with the coming of the gospel, that way of life has now been closed, even if once it was open—and it is doubtful if he would concede even this.[53]

Does Bruce think that Paul in Galatians 3:12 announces the *cessation* of a way to life based on law-keeping, or that Paul is argu-

---

52. Ibid., 28.
53. F. F. Bruce, *The Epistle to the Galatians* (Grand Rapids: Eerdmans, 1982), 163.

ing law-keeping was *never* a way to life? And if the latter, does he think Paul understood or misunderstood the Old Testament text? I do not know.

Bruce's commentary is in general a very fine piece of work; but it is a fallacy to think this sort of equivocal argumentation is actually an explanation of the text.

16. Inadequate analogies

The fallacy in this case lies in supposing that a particular analogy sheds light on a biblical text or theme when in fact that analogy is demonstrably inadequate or inappropriate. Analogies always include elements of both continuity and discontinuity with what they purport to explain; but for an analogy to be worth anything, the elements of continuity must predominate at the point of explanation.

Donald M. Lake, for example, in attempting to argue that grace is no weaker in an Arminian system than in a Reformed system, offers us the analogy of a judge who condemns a guilty criminal and then offers him a pardon.[54] Although the man must accept it, such acceptance, argues Lake, cannot be thought of as a meritorious work, a work that in any sense makes the man deserving of salvation. "Calvin and later Calvinists," he adds, "never seem to be able to see this fundamental distinction unfortunately!"[55]

But to argue that the role of grace in the two systems is not different, Lake would have to change his analogy. He would need to picture a judge rightly condemning ten criminals, and offering each of them pardon. Five of them accept the pardon, the other five reject it (the relative numbers are not important). But in this model, even though those who accept the pardon do not earn it, and certainly enjoy their new freedom because of the judge's "grace," nevertheless they are distinguishable from those who reject the offer solely on the basis of their own decision to accept the pardon. The only thing that separates them from those who are carted off to prison is the wisdom of their

54. Donald M. Lake, "He Died for All: The Universal Dimensions of the Atonement," in *Grace Unlimited,* ed. Clark Pinnock (Minneapolis: Bethany, 1975), 43.
55. Ibid.

own choice. That becomes a legitimate boast. By contrast, in the Calvinistic scheme, the sole determining factor is God's elective grace. Thus, although both systems appeal to grace, the role and place of grace in the two systems are rather different. Lake fails to see this because he has drawn an inadequate analogy; or, more likely, the inadequacy of his chosen analogy demonstrates he has not understood the issue.

17. Abuse of "obviously" and similar expressions

It is perfectly proper for a commentator to use "obviously," "nothing can be clearer," or the like when he or she has marshaled such overwhelming evidence that the vast majority of readers would concur that the matter being presented is transparent, or that the argument is logically conclusive. But it is improper to use such expressions when opposing arguments have not been decisively refuted, and it is a fallacy to think the expressions themselves add anything substantial to the argument.

For instance, when Gleason L. Archer, Jr., seeks to explain why Matthew preserves "poor in spirit" (Matt. 5:3) and Luke simply "poor" (Luke 6:20), he argues that the Sermon on the Mount (Matthew) and the sermon on the plain (Luke) are different discourses. He offers two or three reasons (all of which have been refuted elsewhere), and then concludes, "*Nothing could be clearer* than that these were two different messages delivered at different times."[56] Perhaps he is right; but I remain unpersuaded and have gone on record with the precise opposite of his interpretation.[57] Certainly the majority of commentators, evangelical and otherwise, disagree with Archer on this point. At very least, nothing could be clearer than that "nothing could be clearer" is too strong.

18. Simplistic appeals to authority

Such appeals can be to distinguished scholars, revered pastors, cherished authors, the majority, or various others. The fallacy lies in thinking that appeals to authority constitute reasons

---

56. Gleason L. Archer, Jr., *The Encyclopedia of Bible Difficulties* (Grand Rapids: Zondervan, 1982), 366. Italics added.
57. D. A. Carson, *Matthew* in the *Expositor's Bible Commentary*, ed. Frank E. Gaebelein (Grand Rapids: Zondervan, 1984), in loc.

for interpreting texts a certain way; but in fact, unless that authority's reasons are given, the only thing that such appeals establish is that the writer is under the influence of the relevant authority! The most such an appeal can contribute to an argument is to lend the authority's general reputation to its support; but that is not so much a reasoned defense or explanation as a kind of academic character reference.

Doubtless we should be open to learning from all "authorities" in biblical and theological studies; but we should judge what they say, not on the basis of who said it, but on the basis of the wise reasons they advance.

Here is a fine example from a Roman Catholic writer: "According to the New Testament, Peter has his lapses, both before and after Easter, but Catholic apologists defend the doctrinal infallibility of Peter in the post-Easter situation, and consequently that of the pope in whom the 'Petrine Office' is perpetuated."[58] The appeal is to "Catholic apologists" and implicitly to Roman Catholic traditional interpretations: those not convinced by the status of these authority figures and traditions will not be helped much by Avery Dulles's argument.

These are certainly not the only logical fallacies than can trip up those of us who are intimately involved in the exegesis of the Bible; but they are among the most common. All of us will fall afoul of one or more of these fallacies at some time or another; but alert awareness of their prevalence and nature may help us escape their clutches more frequently than would otherwise be the case.

Like the other chapters of this book, this one is more negative than positive; but if it results in interpreters who are marginally more self-critical in their handling of Scripture, and in readers who are somewhat more discerning when they devour commentaries, expositions, and other studies, this sustained critique will be amply rewarded.

---

58. Avery Dulles, "The Majesterium in History: A Theological Perspective," *ATS Theological Education* 19 (1983): 8.

4

Presuppositional
and Historical Fallacies

The subject of this chapter could easily be turned into a very
long book. To talk about fallacies at the presuppositional and
historical levels is to raise complex questions about philosophy
and history that are beyond my competence and the scope of
this book. Besides, those interested primarily in historical fallacies cannot do better than to read David Hackett Fischer;[1] those
interested in presuppositional fallacies will have to devour substantial quantities of epistemology before they come up with
satisfying comprehensiveness.

Nevertheless, something should be said about presuppositional and historical fallacies in a book like this, for they play a
large role in biblical exegesis. The Bible contains a lot of historical data; and where finite, fallen human beings struggle with
history, there will historians' fallacies be found. Exegesis
involves sustained thought and argumentation; and where there
is such sustained thought, there also will we find presuppositional fallacies.

The Influence of the New Hermeneutic

In the modern climate, it is essential to mention the revolution in
thought brought about by the rise of "the new hermeneutic."[2]

1. David Hackett Fischer, *Historians' Fallacies: Toward a Logic of Historical
Thought* (New York: Harper and Row, 1970).
2. For an introduction, refer to D. A. Carson, "Hermeneutics: A Brief As-
sessment of Some Recent Trends," *Themelios* 5/2 (Jan. 1980): 12–20. More com-

Until a few decades ago, hermeneutics was largely understood to be the art or science of interpretation—as far as theology was concerned, of biblical interpretation. The interpreter is the subject, the text is the object, and the aim in this view is for the subject to develop techniques and "feel" to enable him or her to interpret the object aright. There is much that is laudable in this enterprise; but it does not focus adequately on the barriers to understanding that the interpreter himself brings to the task. At this point the new hermeneutic brings some conceptual light to bear.

The new hermeneutic breaks down the strong subject/object disjunction characteristic of older hermeneutical theory. The interpreter who approaches a text, it is argued, already brings along a certain amount of cultural, linguistic, and ethical baggage. Even the questions the interpreter tries to ask (or fails to ask) of the text reflect the limitations imposed by that baggage; they will in some measure shape the kind of "responses" that can come back from the text and the interpreter's understanding of them. But these responses thereby shape the mental baggage the interpreter is carrying, so that in the next round the kinds of questions addressed to the text will be slightly different, and will therefore generate a fresh series of responses—and so on, and so on. Thus, a "hermeneutical circle" is set up.

In some expositions of the new hermeneutic, real and objective meaning in a text is a mirage, and the pursuit of it as useful as chasing the Cheshire cat. "Polysemy" applied to entire texts is defended in the most naive way—that is, a theory that argues a text has many meanings, none of them objectively true, and all of them valid or invalid according to their effect on the interpreter. But such absolute relativism is not only unnecessary, but also self-contradictory; for the authors of such views expect us to understand the meaning of their articles!

More sophisticated writers understand that the hermeneutical circle is not vicious: ideally, it is more of a hermeneutical spiral. The interpreter can get closer and closer to the meaning of the text (as the writer of that text intended it), until he or she really has grasped it truly, even if not exhaustively. Such writers

---

prehensively, see Anthony C. Thiselton, "The New Hermeneutic," in *New Testament Interpretation: Essays on Principles and Methods,* ed. I. Howard Marshall (Exeter: Paternoster; Grand Rapids: Eerdmans, 1977), 308–33.

deny that a text is cut free from its author as soon as it is written or published: it is always right and valid to ask what the author of the text intended as judged by the indications in the text itself.

In some kinds of literature, of course, there may be a kind of polysemy that *reflects* authorial intent: for example, an aphorism may be designed by its creator to convey truth at several different levels. But such examples do not cut the text off from the author.

Whatever the problems raised by the new hermeneutic, we have learned much from these developments. In particular, we have been forced to recognize that distanciation is an important part of coming to grips with any text: the interpreter must "distance" his or her own horizon of understanding from that of the text. When the differences are more clearly perceived, then it becomes possible to approach the text with greater sensitivity than would otherwise be the case. F. F. Bruce recounts an amusing story of a Christian who did not know anything of distanciation. Apparently this brother, a fisherman, once gave an explanation of why the disciples caught nothing after fishing all night (John 21:3). "They should have known better than to expect anything. We are told that they had with them the two sons of Zebedee. These were the men whom Jesus called the 'sons of thunder,' and it is a fact well known to all fishermen that when there is any thunder in the atmosphere, the fish bury their heads in the sea-bed, and it is impossible to catch any."[3]

In one sense, I have already raised such problems in another guise. In chapter 3, fallacy 5 was labeled "world-view confusion." My focus there was on the logical difficulties involved in reading into the text one's own experiences and concepts; but the same illustrations could be recast to point out these larger problems of presupposition. There are other entries in this chapter that overlap somewhat with entries in the preceding chapter, but I shall try to draw attention to somewhat different phenomena.

If it is true that the new hermeneutic can teach us to be careful and self-conscious about our limitations and prejudices when we approach the Word of God, we will profit greatly; but

3. As related to F. F. Bruce, *In Retrospect: Remembrance of Things Past* (Grand Rapids: Eerdmans, 1980), 11 n. 14.

it will harm us if it serves as a ground for the relativizing of all opinion about what Scripture is saying. I do not know what biblical authority means, nor even what submission to the lordship of Jesus Christ means, if we are unprepared to bend our opinions, values, and mental structures to what the Bible says, to what Jesus teaches. There may be differences of opinion about what the Bible is in fact saying, differences that can sometimes be resolved with humble interaction and much time; but among Christians there should be little excuse for ignoring or avoiding what the Bible has to say, on the false grounds that knowledge of objective truth is impossible.

More recently, the "new hermeneutic" has been displaced in many circles by "radical hermeneutics." With complex roots in linguistics and structuralism, radical hermeneutics has fostered an array of interpretive approaches (the best known of which is deconstruction) that are grounded in postmodern epistemology. Rejecting "modern" epistemology with its insistence on foundations and proper method, postmodernists, sometimes on highly sophisticated grounds, argue that there are no secure foundations, and all methods are themselves theory-laden. The result is that there is no univocal, authoritative "meaning" in the text itself. If one must use the word "meaning" of a text, one should speak of the "meanings" of the text—that is, the different meanings that different individuals or different interpretive communities will find there. Indeed, properly speaking the meanings are not really in the text itself but in the interpreters of the text, as they interact with it.

The issues are so complex it would be impractical to deal with them here.[4] But perhaps a few observations on some hermeneutical fallacies may be helpful, even if I do not here attempt to ground my observations in detailed argument.

1. Fallacies arising from omission of distanciation in the interpretative process

The most obvious of these is reading one's personal theology into the text. We might grin at Bruce's story of the fisher-

---

4. For substantial bibliography and some preliminary wrestling with the issue, see D. A. Carson, *The Gagging of God: Christianity Confronts Pluralism* (Grand Rapids: Zondervan Publishing House, 1995).

man; but Protestants must ask themselves if the "you are Peter" passage (Matt. 16:13–20) would find interpreters scrambling to identify the rock not with Peter but with his confession, his faith, or his Lord, if there had not been many centuries of papal claims falsely based on that passage. Our presuppositions, called up by an error on the other side, do not easily give way to modification by the biblical text. The problem becomes even more acute when it is not the interpreter's tradition that is at stake so much as a cherished point in the interpreter's personal theology—perhaps even a published point!

But if we sometimes read our own theology into the text, the solution is not to retreat to an attempted neutrality, to try to make one's mind a tabula rasa so we may listen to the text without bias. It cannot be done, and it is a fallacy to think it can be. We must rather discern what our prejudices are and make allowances for them; and meanwhile we should learn all the historical theology we can. One well-known seminary insists that proper exegetical method will guarantee such a high quality of exegesis that historical theology may be safely ignored. I can think of no better way of cultivating the soil that sprouts either heresy or the shallowest sort of traditionalism. Perhaps one of the most intriguing—and disturbing—features of Zane C. Hodges's book,[5] to which reference has already been made, is that to the best of my knowledge not one significant interpreter of Scripture in the entire history of the church has held to Hodges's pattern of interpretation of the passages he treats.

This is not to say there are no other interpreters in the history of the church who have not entertained one kind or another of two-step salvation, or who have not entertained some distinction between accepting Jesus as Savior and accepting Jesus as Lord. But I know no one who pursues this track with the rigor of Hodges, resulting in many, many utterly novel (and, I fear, unconvincing) exegeses. One of the best brief treatments of the issues involved is provided by John Piper.[6]

5. Zane C. Hodges, *The Gospel under Siege: A Study on Faith and Works* (Dallas: Redención Villa, 1981).
6. *The Pleasures of God* (Portland: Multnomah, 1991), 279–305.

2. Interpretations that ignore the Bible's story-line

Precisely because so many interpreters do not hold that there is an omniscient God who actually stands behind all of the Bible, they feel free to read parts of it in ways that are deliberately set over against other parts of the Bible. Postmodern biases have accentuated this trend. Thus it has been argued that Song of Solomon is an instance of pornographic literature;[7] that James and Paul are utterly irreconcilable; that the Gospels reflect not only different communities but irreconcilable differences among those communities; and much more of the same. Many recent books have as their primary aim the articulation of as many mutually competing interpretations as possible.[8] The only incorrect view is the view that any view should be labeled incorrect; the only heresy is the view that there is such a thing as heresy.

Christians who have a high view of Scripture, a commitment to truth because they serve a God who knows all truth perfectly, and who recognize that although in our finiteness and sinfulness we may not know truth absolutely or perfectly but nevertheless truly, will not want to go down such paths. They will be interested in discovering how the Bible fits together. For fit together it does, tracing its way along a story-line from the creation and fall, through great redemptive-historical appointments to the consummation in a new heaven and a new earth.

3. Fallacies that arise from a bleak insistence on working outside the Bible's "givens"

This is painfully common today. The current social agenda is taken as the assumed "given" and the text is made to conform to it. Postmoderns see nothing wrong with this procedure; indeed, they are inclined to think it is inevitable. But the result is often fantastic.

7. David J. A. Clines, "Why Is There a Song of Songs and What Does It Do to You When You Read It?" *Jian Dao* 1 (1994): 3–27.
8. E.g., J. Cheryl Exum and David J. A. Clines, *The New Literary Criticism and the Hebrew Bible* (Valley Forge: Trinity Press International, 1993); David Seeley, *Deconstructing the New Testament* (Leiden: E. J. Brill, 1994); Stephen D. Moore, *Mark and Luke in Poststructuralist Perspectives: Jesus Begins to Write* (New Haven: Yale University Press, 1992); Francis Watson, ed., *The Open Text: New Directions for Biblical Studies?* (London: SCM Press, 1993).

For example, Castelli argues that when a powerful figure such as Paul urges that others imitate him (1 Cor. 11:1), this is always a power move that splits people into insiders and outsiders, conformists and nonconformists. Such urging is inherently a political move that privileges a certain view of reality and marginalizes others who disagree. The appeal for unity becomes a pretext to justify hegemony. What we should be doing, rather, is reinstating the value of difference.[9]

All of this presupposes that the God of the Bible does not exist, or that if he exists he has no inclination to demand that his image-bearers live in a certain way, and not in other ways. The self-confidence with which the value of unqualified "difference" is put forth is staggering, and staggeringly naive. But this sort of interpretation is no longer uncommon.

Historical Fallacies

1. Uncontrolled historical reconstruction

The fallacy is in thinking that speculative reconstruction of first-century Jewish and Christian history should be given much weight in the exegesis of the New Testament documents. A substantial block of New Testament scholars have traced a network of theological trajectories to explain how the church changed its thinking from decade to decade and from place to place. The church was once "enthusiastic" and charismatic, then settled into "early catholicism" with its structures, hierarchies, formulas, and creeds. It looked forward at one time to the impending return of Christ, only to be forced by his continued absence to construct a theory of a delayed parousia and settle down for the long haul. It began in a Jewish context by calling Jesus the Messiah and ended in a Gentile context by calling him Lord and ascribing deity to him.

Now there is just enough truth in this reconstruction that it cannot simply be written off. The Book of Acts itself demonstrates how the church came to wrestle with the place of Gentiles in the fledgling messianic community, faced the problem of the relation between the Mosaic covenant of law and the gos-

9. Elizabeth A. Castelli, *Imitating Paul: A Discourse of Power* (Louisville: Westminster/John Knox Press, 1991).

pel of grace in Christ Jesus, and learned to adapt its presentation of the good news to new contexts. Nevertheless the reconstruction of church history that is held by many biblical scholars goes much further, and concludes, for instance, that the references to elders in Acts and the Pastorals prove those documents are late, because elders belong to the "early catholic" period of the church. Again and again the New Testament documents are squeezed into this reconstructed history and assessed accordingly.

The problem is that we have almost no access to the history of the early church during its first five or six decades *apart* from the New Testament documents. A little speculative reconstruction of the flow of history is surely allowable if we are attempting to fill in some of the lacunae left by insufficient evidence; but it is methodologically indefensible to use those speculations to undermine large parts of the only evidence we have. If a scholar feels that some of that evidence is unreliable or misleading, then the canons of scholarship afford him or her every opportunity to make a case for disregarding that evidence; but it is a fallacy to think that speculative reconstructions have any force in overturning the evidence. It is far wiser for a scholar who discounts some piece of evidence to make the best possible case for that judgment and then admit he does not know what really did happen historically, or even venture some cautious speculation about what happened, than to try to use the speculation itself as a telling point to throw out the evidence.

This problem is so endemic to New Testament scholarship that many of the divisions between conservative and liberal scholars can be traced to this methodological fallacy. I see no possibility of substantial movement unless this problem is directly addressed.

Worse yet, this uncontrolled historical reconstruction is often linked with the more extravagant approaches to form criticism to produce double uncontrolled work.[10] To cite but one example, in his treatment of the parable of the ten virgins (Matt.

10. I have outlined some of the inherent weakness of form and redaction criticism as commonly practiced in contemporary New Testament studies in "Redaction Criticism: On the Use and Abuse of a Literary Tool," in *Scripture and Truth*, ed. D. A. Carson and John D. Woodbridge (Grand Rapids: Zondervan, 1983), 119–42, 376–81.

25:1–13) Rudolf Bultmann makes a number of preliminary observations and then comments, "It is no longer possible to decide whether an original Similitude underlies it. Its content—the delay of the Parousia—also reveals that it is a secondary formulation."[11] Thus, the least defensible elements of form criticism combine with the most speculative historical reconstruction to form critical judgments absolutely devoid of substantive evidence.

2. Fallacies of causation

Fallacies of causation are faulty explanations of the causes of events. Fischer lists quite a few,[12] including *post hoc, propter hoc*, "the mistaken idea that if event B happened after event A, it happened because of event A";[13] *cum hoc, propter hoc*, which "mistakes correlation for cause";[14] *pro hoc, propter hoc*, "putting the effect before the cause";[15] the reductive fallacy, which "reduces complexity to simplicity, or diversity to uniformity, in causal explanations";[16] the fallacy of reason as cause, which "mistakes a causal for a logical order, or vice versa";[17] and the fallacy of responsibility as cause, which "confuses a problem of ethics with a problem of agency in a way which falsifies both."[18]

It is not difficult to find examples of these and other fallacies in the writings of New Testament scholars. Granted that Edwin M. Yamauchi and others are right in arguing that there is no good evidence of full-blown Gnosticism in the pre-Christian period,[19] it is difficult to resist the conclusion that a great many

11. Rudolf Bultmann, *History of the Synoptic Tradition* (New York: Harper and Row, 1963), 176. This book boasts combinations like this on almost every page.

12. Fischer, *Historians' Fallacies*, 164–82.

13. Ibid., 166.

14. Ibid., 167.

15. Ibid., 169.

16. Ibid., 172.

17. Ibid., 180.

18. Ibid., 182.

19. See especially Edwin M. Yamauchi, *Pre-Christian Gnosticism: A Survey of the Proposed Evidences*, 2d ed. (Grand Rapids: Baker, 1983), and his excellent review of James M. Robinson, ed., *The Nag Hammadi Library* (San Francisco: Harper and Row, 1978) in "Pre-Christian Gnosticism in the Nag Hammadi Texts?" *Church History* 48 (1979): 129–41.

of the connections drawn by scholars (especially those of the "history of religions school") who believe Christianity is an off-shoot of Gnosticism are nothing more than examples of *pro hoc, propter hoc*, the worst kind of causal fallacy. Of course, a more charitable interpretation of their opinions would point out that those who hold them believe Gnosticism is in fact pre-Christian, and therefore their connections are not examples of the *pro hoc, propter hoc* fallacy. Even so, many such connections then fall afoul of the *post hoc, propter hoc* fallacy until the connection has been rigorously established.

An example of *cum hoc, propter hoc* that occurs frequently in evangelical preaching runs as follows: Paul in his Athenian address (Acts 17:22–31) erred in trying to approach his hearers philosophically rather than biblically, and his own acknowledgment of his error turned up in 1 Corinthians, where he pointed out that at Corinth, the next stop after Athens, he resolved to know nothing while he was with them except Jesus Christ and him crucified (1 Cor. 2:2). This exegesis seriously misunderstands the address at the Areopagus and Luke's purpose in telling it; but it also connects pieces of information from two separate documents and without evidence affirms a causal connection: because Paul allegedly failed miserably in Athens, therefore he resolved to return to his earlier practice. In fact, there is a geographical and temporal correlation (Paul did travel to Corinth from Athens), but not a shred of evidence for causation.

3. Fallacies of motivation

Again, it is Fischer who most ably lays these out.[20] Motivational fallacies might be considered a subset of causal fallacies: "Motivational explanation might be understood as a special kind of causal explanation in which the effect is an intelligent act and the cause is the thought behind it. Or it might be conceived in noncausal terms, as a paradigm of patterned behavior."[21]

I shall not list an array of such fallacies. All of them have to do with explaining a certain historical development on the basis of specific choices and preferences. In the worst cases, it is an

20. Fischer, *Historians' Fallacies*, 187–215.
21. Ibid., 187.

attempt to psychoanalyze one or more of the participants in a past event, without having access to the patient—indeed, without having access to anything more than fragmentary records of the event.

The highest proportion of motivational fallacies crops up today in some radical redaction critical study of the New Testament. Every redactional change must have a *reason* behind it; so enormous creative energy is spent providing such reasons. They are most difficult to disprove; but apart from those cases where the text itself provides rich and unambiguous evidence, they are rarely more than raw speculation. For instance, because Robert H. Gundry holds that Matthew's birth narratives are dependent on Luke, he feels he must explain every change. The Magi meet Jesus in a house (2:11–12), not a stable, because a stable is "hardly a fit place for distinguished Magi [whom Gundry does not think are historical anyway] to offer expensive gifts to a king."[22] In other words, Gundry simply asserts that the reason Matthew changed "stable" to "house" is to accommodate a theological motif. Gundry, of course, has no independent access to Matthew's mind: he only has the text of this Gospel. Yet he is prepared to elucidate Matthew's reason, his motives, for this putative change, and for literally thousands more cases solely on the basis of a certain redaction critical theory. I am not very sanguine about the results.[23]

4. Conceptual parallelomania

This is a conceptual counterpart to the verbal parallelomania I treated in chapter 1. Moisés Silva lists some examples from Edith Hamilton's book about Greek culture.[24] She describes Sophoclean tragedy in the words "Lo, I come . . . to do thy will" (Heb. 10:7, KJV, citing Ps. 40:6–8, LXX); and Ephesians 6:12 ("For our struggle is not against flesh and blood," NIV) becomes in her hands an illustration of the fact that the most divisive

22. Robert H. Gundry, *Matthew: A Commentary on His Literary and Theological Art* (Grand Rapids: Eerdmans, 1982), 31.

23. See the review of Gundry's commentary in *Trinity Journal* 3 (1982): 71–91.

24. Moisés Silva, "The New Testament Use of the Old Testament: Text Form and Authority," in *Scripture and Truth*, ed. D. A. Carson and John D. Woodbridge (Grand Rapids: Zondervan, 1983), 157.

human conflicts are those waged "for one side of the truth to the suppression of the other side."[25] Conceptual parallelomania is particularly inviting to those who have taken advanced training in a specialized field (psychology, sociology, some area of history, philosophy, education) but who have no more than a serious Sunday-school knowledge of the Scriptures. Many of the specialists who fall into these fallacies are devout believers who want to relate the Bible to their discipline. They think they have a much firmer grasp of Scripture than they do; and the result is frequently appalling nonsense.

25. Edith Hamilton, *The Greek Way* (1930; New York: Avon, 1973), 187, 247.

5

Concluding Reflections

At this stage I do not propose to start listing more fallacies, but to prime the pump of future discussion by briefly listing some areas where more opportunities for fallacies lurk in the darkness to catch the unwary. This list is not comprehensive, merely suggestive.

Opportunities for Even More Fallacies

1. Problems related to literary genre

There are many. Our modern definitions of "parable" or "allegory" may not be quite what ancient writers meant by these terms. The new hermeneutic has established much of its theory by studying parables, which in Jesus' hands were often meant to shock and "interpret" the hearer to himself, as much as to be interpreted by the hearer; but the theories work less well in a tractate letter or a discourse. How may we shape our questions about genre by the genre being studied? Again, many studies in this area fall afoul of the need for evenhanded balancing of continuities *and discontinuities* when two pieces of literature are being compared.

One of the most common errors preachers make in the area of literary genre occurs in their handling of Proverbs. A proverb is neither a promise nor case law. If it is treated that way, it may prove immensely discouraging to some believers when things do not seem to work out as the "promise" seeks to suggest.

Perhaps the easiest way of making the point is by comparing two proverbs that are located side by side. "Do not answer a fool according to his folly," Proverbs 26:4 pronounces. The next verse adds, "Answer a fool according to his folly." The second part of each verse helps us sort out this strange conjunction:

> Do not answer a fool according to his folly,
> or you will be like him yourself (26:4).
>
> Answer a fool according to his folly,
> or he will be wise in his own eyes (26:5).

A thoughtful reader will have to ask when it is best to follow one verse or the other. That question will prompt reflection on the second line of each verse: Will my "foolish" response be bringing me down to the other's level (26:4), or will it be pricking the other's pretensions and warning him of his course (26:5)? How can I tell?

In other words, proverbs often demand meditation, subtle reflection on the circumstances under which the proverb applies, recognition that the proverb provides us with God-given wisdom on how to live under the fear of God, rather than simplistic univocal promises or the like.

Similarly, the careful interpreter will work through the way Hebrew poetry, apocalyptic, historical passages, gospels, laments, and many other forms, actually work—how they convey meaning and truth, how they bring encouragement or instruction or warning, and so forth.

2. Problems related to the New Testament use of the Old

These include the nature of the Old Testament's authority when the connection is typological, the danger of a purely fideistic appeal in the difficult passages, the question of whether (and when) the quotation is meant to bring the Old Testament context with it, and much more. These problems all invite fallacies of various kinds.

3. Arguments from silence

One reviewer of James B. Hurley's book on the roles of men and women criticized it rather severely for not adequately considering the silences of Jesus regarding limitations on women.[1]

---

1. Linda Merandante, writing about James B. Hurley, *Man and Woman in Biblical Perspective* (Grand Rapids: Zondervan, 1981), in *TSF Bull* 6 (Jan.–Feb. 1983): 21–22.

Scholars usually recognize that arguments from silence are weak; but they are stronger if a case can be made that in any particular context we might have expected further comment from the speaker or narrator. My purpose is not to arbitrate this particular dispute, but to point out that various fallacies can attach themselves either to arguments from silence or to the construction of contexts used to give arguments from silence some force.

4. Problems relating to juxtapositions of texts

Some of these are forced to the surface when we consider the Arian efforts to link John 10:30 ("I and the Father are one," NIV) and John 17:20–23 ("I pray . . . that all of them may be one, Father, just as you are in me and I am in you," NIV). What gives interpreters the right to link certain verses together, and not others? The point is that all such linking eventually produces a grid that affects the interpretation of other texts. There may be fallacies connected not only with the way individual verses are interpreted, but also with the way several passages are linked— and then also with the way such a link affects the interpretation of the next verse that is studied!

For instance, it is difficult to resist the conclusion that George W. Knight's treatment of 1 Corinthians 14:33b–38, regarding the silence of women in the churches, requires that the Corinthian readers had already read 1 Timothy 2:11–15, which on any chronology was not yet written; for Knight himself, recognizing that in the light of 1 Corinthians 11:5 the silence referred to in 1 Corinthians 14:34 cannot be absolute, appeals to 1 Timothy 2:11–15 to find appropriate limitations to the prohibition.[2] Other approaches are possible; but in any case a rationale is needed for this particular (or any other) juxtaposition of texts on which so much is made to depend.

I do not propose to offer tentative methodological solutions to such problems; but it is quite clear that many of the disputes in Christianity—whether long-standing debates over the relation between God's sovereignty and man's responsibility, or more recent foci of interest such as the relationships between

---

2. George W. Knight III, *The New Testament Teaching on the Role Relationship of Men and Women* (Grand Rapids: Baker, 1977), 36–40.

men and women in the Christian church—revolve around inconsistencies, errors, and fallacies in this area. The kinds of fallacies involved are very often of the sort that have already been treated in this book; the application of what we have learned to problems of constructing a consistent biblical theology would take us into new twists and turns of thought that stand beyond the reach of this book. Certainly a great deal more work needs to be done in this area.

5. *Problems relating to statistical arguments*

Many exegetical judgments are shaped in part by redaction critical decisions that depend on numbers—the frequency with which a certain word or phrase occurs in a specified corpus, whether it occurs in unambiguously redactional material or elsewhere, and so forth.

But there are many methodological fallacies connected with statistical arguments, fallacies of which most New Testament scholars are only vaguely aware. For instance, many redactional decisions are based on counts of words that occur only four or five times. Statistically it can be shown that the possibility of error in such judgment calls is 50 percent, 70 percent, 80 percent, or even higher. Moreover, word frequency statistics are normally calculated on the basis of the null hypothesis. This statistical model figures out how likely various occurrences would be in comparison with a random drawing of words out of a barrel. But writers do not choose words that way. There may be convincing contextual or topical reasons why some words are chosen in one context and not in another.

More serious yet, too few studies have been done in comparative literature to know if there are standard patterns of variability within the writings of one author. If enough of such studies were done (and ideally it would take thousands), we could eliminate our reliance on the null hypothesis.

Again, most redaction critical judgments treat "redactional" words and phrases, and sometimes the passages in which they are embedded, as late additions or as references to nonhistorical material. But statistical tests have never been done to determine how often other writers (e.g., Josephus) use their own words and combine them with sources at their disposal to relate matters that are historical. Such comparative studies are sadly lacking.

6. The rise of structuralism[3]

A new generation of fallacies is in the process of being created as this relatively young discipline is applied to biblical studies.

7. Problems in distinguishing the figurative and the literal

It is quite common to find interpretations that mistake the literal for the figurative, or vice versa. The theology of some cults *depends* on such misreadings. James W. Sire points out that Christian Science offers figurative interpretations of scores of biblical words, without offering exegetical justification (e.g., "dove" is a symbol for divine Science, purity, and peace; "evening" symbolizes "instances of mortal thought; weariness of mortal mind; obscured view; peace and rest"), and Mormonism offers a literal interpretation of many apparently figurative uses of words (e.g., God must have a body because the text speaks of God's strong right arm).[4] But what are the controlling principles for determining figurative/literal distinctions? A good place to begin such study is G. B. Caird's book;[5] but in any case the problem offers another fertile field for fallacies of exegesis.

Bringing the Pieces Together

This discussion has necessarily treated fallacies piecemeal; but in the actual work of exegesis, some passages by their sheer complexity stir up a multiplicity of fallacies at the same time—in the same way that the law stirs up sin. I think of passages such as Psalm 110; Isaiah 52:13–53:12; Matthew 16:13–23; Ephesians 5:21–30; and Revelation 20:1–6.

Then on top of the strictly exegetical fallacies, we face new dangers when we seek to apply to our lives the meaning of the text we have discovered—that is, when we ask how the Bible is

3. For an easy introduction to what "structuralism" means, refer to J. P. Louw, *Semantics of New Testament Greek* (Philadelphia: Fortress; Chico, Calif.: Scholars Press, 1982), 91–158. For more detailed bibliography of the standard discussions, see D. A. Carson, "Hermeneutics," *Themelios* 5/2 (Jan. 1980): 12–20.

4. James W. Sire, *Scripture Twisting: Twenty Ways the Cults Misread the Bible* (Downers Grove, Ill.: Inter-Varsity, 1980), 66–70.

5. G. B. Caird, *The Language and Imagery of the Bible* (London: Duckworth, 1980).

to be used.[6] May we take any narrative paradigmatically? Must interpretations of discrete passages be related to salvation-historical wholeness? More practically, is footwashing an institution for the church to observe? Identifying and avoiding fallacies related to such questions would require quite a different book.

But I do not want to end on so negative a note. There is a danger that readers will conclude their perusal of this little book enslaved to deep fears about their own inadequacies for the task of exegesis. A little self-doubt will do no harm and may do a great deal of good: we will be more open to learn and correct our mistakes. But too much will shackle and stifle us with deep insecurities and make us so much aware of methods that we may overlook truth itself.

I have no easy answer to this dilemma. But we will not go far astray if we approach the Bible with a humble mind and then resolve to focus on central truths. Gradually we will build up our exegetical skills by evenhanded study and a reverent, prayerful determination to become like the workman "who correctly handles the word of truth" (1 Tim. 2:15, NIV).

6. See David H. Kelsey, *The Uses of Scripture in Recent Theology* (Philadelphia: Fortress, 1975).

Index of Subjects

Allegorical method, 90
Ambiguous language, 119–20
Anachronism, semantic, 33–35
Analogy, inadequate, 121–22
Aorist tense, 68–75
Aphorism, 127
Apodoses, 78–79
Appeals to authority, simplistic, 122–23
Article, Greek, definite, 79–84
Associative jumps, unwarranted, 115–16
Assumptions, false, 45–47

Background material, 41–43, 57
Baconian fallacy, 104–5

Causation, fallacies of, 133–34
Cavalier dismissal, 118
Classical Greek, 32, 37, 66
Componential analysis, 49–50
Computer technology, 20
Conditionals, 77–79
Context, 32, 57, 64; of Greek words in the aorist tense, 71
Contextualization, 20
Copula usage, 58–60: attributes in, 58, 59–60; cause in, 58; fulfillment in, 60; identity in, 58–60; resemblance in, 58
Cum hoc, propter hoc, 133–34
Crowell rule, 82–84
Cruces interpretum, 120

Deliberate subjunctive, 74–75
Denotation, 63–64
Discernment, spiritual, 16
Disjunction: false, 90–92; semantic, 55–57; subject/object, 126
Distanciation, 23–24, 104, 128–29

Emotive appeals, 106–8
Entropy, in language, 66
Equivalence, 47–48
Equivocal argumentation, 118–21
Etymology, 33. See also Word study and Words
Evidence, selective and prejudicial use of, 54–55, 93–94
Excluded middle, law of, 90–92, 103
Exegesis, conflicting, 17, 18–20; critical, 16–17; and hermeneutics, 25; role of teachers in, 20
Exegetical fallacies: danger of studying, 22–24; importance of, 15–22; frequency of, 15–16
Expanded semantic field, unwarranted use of, 60–61

False statements, 116–17
Figurative language, 141
Form criticism, 132–33

Generalization, unwarranted, 108–15
Genre, literary, 137–38
GRAMCORD, 73, 85
Grammar, 20, 65–68
Grammatical analysis, 65–66
Granville Sharp rule, 81–82
Greek, New Testament: 33, 66–67; and classical Greek, 32, 35, 37, 66; flexibility of, 66; and Hebrew equivalents, 61–62; ostentatious use of, 64; tenses in, 67–73
"Greek mind," 44

Hebrew language and thought, 33, 48, 54
"Hebrew mind," 44–45
Hellenistic Greek. See Greek, New Testament
Hendiadys, 42

Hapax legomena, 33
Hermeneutics, 20, 25
Historical reconstruction, 131–33
Holy Spirit, and exegesis, 16, 26
Hyponymic relations, 48

Illegitimate totality transfer, 53. *See
also* Expanded semantic field
Imprecision, and truth, 106

Jumps, associative, unwarranted,
115–16
Juxtaposition of texts, 139–40

Linguistics, 20
Linkage, of language and mentality,
44–45
Literal interpretation, 141
Literary studies, 20
Logic, nature and universality of, 87–
90

Metaphors, 57
Middle voice, 75–77
Motivation, fallacies of 134–35

Negative inferences, 101–3
Negativism, 22
New Hermeneutic, 125–28
Non sequitur, 117–18

Obsolescence, semantic, 35–37
Obviously, abuse of the word, 122
Old Testament, use of in the New Testament, 138
Open options, 120–21
Overspecification, 115

Parallelomania: conceptual, 135–36;
verbal, 43–44
Peculiarities of a corpus, neglect of, 62
Periphrasis, 62, 126
Philology, 27
Polysemy, 126–27

Pro hoc, propter hoc, 133–34
Protases, 77–79

Question-framing, 105–6

"Radical" hermeneutics, 128
Redaction criticism, 135, 140
Referential meaning, 63–64
Restriction, of semantic field, 57–60
Rhetorical questions, 118–19
Root fallacy, 28–33, 51

Scriptures: authority of, 21; high view
of, 19, 130; trustworthiness of, 21
Semitic languages and background,
58, 61, 62
Septuagint, 62
Silence, argument from, 138–39
Social agendas, and exegetical fallacies, 130
Statistics, argument from, 140
Story-line, of the Bible, 130
Structuralism, 141
Syllogism, 94–103
Synonyms 47–53
Synonymy. *See* Synonyms

Technical meaning, 45–47, 57
Tenses, in the Greek language, 67–75;
relationships of, 84–85
Terminus technicus. See Technical
meaning

Unknown or unlikely meanings, 37–
41

Word study: breadth of, 64; paradigmatic, 64
Words: components of, 32; context of,
32; diachronic study of, 33; lexical
range of, 32; related to meaning,
32; semantic range of, 32, 57–58
World-view fallacy, 103–5

Index of Authors

Albright, W. F., 88
Archer, Gleason L., Jr., 117n46, 122

Barclay, William, 29
Barr, James, 21, 27n1, 30, 44
Barrett, C. K., 102
Barth, C., 91n9
Bauer, 37
Bedale, S., 38
Belleville, Linda L., 42
Bornkamm, G., 91n9
Bowman, T., 44n42
Boyer, James L., 78, 85
Brand, Paul, 34n
Brooks, James, A., 75n12, 81n19
Brown, Harold O. J., 120
Bruce, F. F., 120, 127n
Bruner, Frederick Dale, 46n48
Bultmann, Rudolf, 43, 133

Caird, G. B., 27n1, 36n22, 58–59, 141
Calvin, John, 89, 102
Carson, D. A., 43nn36, 39, 47nn52 ,
    53, 60nn78, 79, 82n22, 89n, 99n21,
    106n, 107n36, 108, 112n, 122n57,
    125n2, 128n, 132n, 135n24, 141n3,
Castelli, Elizabeth A., 131
Caton, Charles E., 63n89
Chantry, Walter J., 108, 110
Clark, Stephen B., 93n, 110, 112
Clines, David J. A., 130nn7, 8
Colwell, E. C., 82–84,
Conzelmann, Hans, 118n50
Cranfield, C. E. B., 38

Dahms, John V., 31n, 88
Dewey, Ed, 84
Dodd, C. H., 43
Downs, Perry G., 54n66
Drane, John W., 105n33
Dulles, Avery, 123n

Exum, J. Cheryl, 130n8

Fanning, Buist, 67n
Fee, Gordon D., 99n21
Fischer, David Hackett, 20, 21n4,
    104–5, 125, 133n11–18, 134,
Fitzmyer, Joseph A., 38n26
France, R.T, 43n39

Gaebelein, Frank E., 77n
Geisler, Norman L., 45n, 88
Gibson, Arthur, 27n1, 44, 48, 88
Goetchius, E. V. N., 84n27
Grassmick, John D., 90
Groome, Thomas H., 54–55, 117
Grudem, Wayne A., 37n25, 41n, 93n,
    106, 108n37
Gundry, Robert H., 21, 135

Hamilton, Edith, 135–36n
Hare, D. R. A., 47n51
Harrington, D. J., 47n51
Harris, Murray J., 83n24
Hatch, Edwin, 61
Headlam, Arthur C., 70n7
Held, H. J., 91
Hendriksen, William, 52–53
Hodges, Zane C., 91–92, 100, 129
Hoeldtke, Clyde, 55n68
Hofmann, J. B., 29
Hollenweger, Walter J., 46n47
Homer, 29
Horton, Michael Scott, 107n36
Hughes, Philip Edgcumbe, 70
Hurley, James B., 38n27, 41n, 56n69,
    93n, 138

Jerome, 31
Johnston, Robert K., 18
Joly, Robert, 51–52nn62, 63
Josephus, 140

Kaiser, Walter C., Jr., 38, 41
Kelsey, David H., 142
Kilgore, William J., 88n1
Knight, George W. III, 139
Kysar, Robert, 43

Lake, Donald, M., 121n
Leitch, James, W., 118n50
Lenski, R. C. H., 56, 70, 81n18, 99
Louw, J. P., 27n1, 29–30n11, 62n85, 141n3
Lyons, John, 48n58

MacRae, George W., 118n50
Malherbe, A. J., 27n2
Mare, W. Harold, 77n
Marshall, I. Howard, 28n4, 84, 126n
Martin, Ralph, 47n53
McComiskey, Thomas E., 63n88
McGaughy, Lane C., 84
McKay, Kenneth L., 67n, 70n4
McKim, Donald, 89
Merandante, Linda, 138n
Mickelsen, Alvera, 37–38, 41
Mickelsen, Berkeley, 37–38, 41
Miller, Paul, 85
Miranda, José, 120
Moo, Douglas J., 38n29, 70n7, 94
Moody, Dale, 31n
Moore, Stephen D., 130n8
Morris, Leon, 29, 41, 42n32, 51n60, 90
Moulton, James Hope, 75n13, 83n26
Murray, Iain, 46n50

Nash, Ronald, 98n19
Nida, Eugene A., 27n1, 32n1, 49n
Nix, William E., 45n

Odeberg, Hugo, 41–42

Payne, Philip B., 94
Pinnock, Clark, 121
Piper, John, 129
Porter, Stanley E., 67n, 79n
Przybylski, Benno, 62

Räisänen, Heikki, 70
Ramm, Bernard, 16n1
Richards, Lawrence O., 55–56, 108n, 109

Robertson, A. T., 29, 75n12, 81n20
Robinson, J. Armitage, 66
Robinson, James M., 133n19
Rogers, Jack B., 89
Rydbeck, Lars, 85n
Ryle, Gilbert, 63

Sanday, William, 70n7
Sanders, J. T., 48–49, 96–98
Sandmel, Samuel, 43
Satchitananda, Swami, 103
Seeley, David, 130n8
Sharp, Granville, 81–82
Silva, Moisés, 27n1, 33, 44, 49n, 61, 63n87, 135
Sire, James W., 103, 115n, 141
Smith, Charles R., 70, 101
Söderblom, Nathan, 27
Stagg, Frank, 68–70
Steinmetz, David C., 92–93, 107
Stibbs, Alan, 35n19

Taber, Charles R., 27n1
Terry, Milton S., 57n72
Thiselton, Anthony C., 28, 126n
Toon, Peter, 47n53
Toussaint, Stanley D., 76n14
Trench, R. C., 29, 35n20
Trites, Alison A., 36n22
Turner, Nigel, 61, 83n26

Ullmann, Stephen, 27n1, 33n15, 35n21, 48n58

van Veen, J. M., 27n2
von Balthasar, Hans Urs, 98n20, 99

Walker, Rolf, 47n51
Watson, Francis, 130n8
Wenham, David, 43n39
Winbery, Carlton L., 75n12, 81n19
Woodbridge, John D., 89n, 106n, 132n, 135n24
Wuest, Kenneth S., 117

Yamauchi, Edwin M., 133
Yancey, Philip, 34n

Zerwick, Maximillian, 91n10

Index of Scripture

Genesis

2:20b–24 40
25:1–2 31

Leviticus

18:5 120

2 Samuel

13 (LXX) 31
13:15 (LXX) 31

Psalms

22:20 (21:21, LXX) 30
25:16 (24:16, LXX) 31, 31n
40:6–8 (LXX) 135
110 141

Proverbs

26:4 137, 138
26:5 138

Song of Solomon

Book of 130

Isaiah

52:13–53:12 141

Jeremiah

1:5 115

Ezekiel

36:25–27 42

Matthew

1:21 101n25

2:11–12 135
4:15 47
5:1 42, 43
5:3 122
5:8 103
5:17–20 60
5:20 62
6:6 68
6:32 47
7:12 60
7:21–23 113
10:5 47
10:18 47
11:11–13 60
12:18 47
12:21 47
12:27 77
16:1 81, 82
16:6 81, 82
16:11 82
16:12 82
16:13–20 129
16:13–23 141
18:13 79
20:16 63
20:19 47
20:25 47
21:43 47
22:14 63
24:9 47
24:14 47
24:24 113, 114
25:1–13 132–33
25:32 47
26:46 76
27:5 76
28:18 56, 116
28:18–20 46
28:19 47

Mark

1:11 69

3:24–25 79
6:24 75
10:17–27 110
10:18 58
10:38 76
12:14 74

Luke

2:5 76
6:17 42, 43
6:20 122
7:12 31n
8:24 77
8:42 31n
9:38 31n
10:7 80
20:13 74
22:47 52

John

1:1 59, 60, 82, 83, 84
1:1–18 43
3:3 42
3:5 41, 42, 42n
3:6 42
3:6b 42
3:7 42
3:10 42
3:11–21 99
3:16 31, 31n, 99
3:17 99
3:35 32
4:50 55
5:20 32
5:47 55
11:26 55
13:19 55
14:6 100
14:6b 100
15:4 56n71

15:14 56
17:11 56
17:20–23 139
17:21 55
20:21 116, 117
20:28 60
21:3 117, 127
21:15–17 52

Acts

Book of 131
2:16 60
2:17 93
6:1–6 94, 95
7:38 61
17:18 82
17:22–31 134
18:9–10 114n
20 113
21:9 93
21:32 77
23:7 82

Romans

1:16 34
3:21 38
3:21–26 35
3:24 35
3:27 70
5:6–9 35
5:12 68, 69
6:15 75
7:7 58
8:6 58
10:9 96, 97
10:9–10 96, 98
12:1 68

1 Corinthians

1:2 45
2:2 134

3 99
3:21ff 98
4:1 29
4:6 115
5:7 68, 69
6:12 39
7:1–2 39
7:18 110
7:19 112
7:21a 112
7:21b 112
7:40b 40
9:19–23 112, 112n
11:1 131
11:2–15 94
11:2–16 37, 38, 40, 93
11:3 38n26
11:4–6 118
11:5 139
11:8–9 40
11:16 40
12:3 101
12:13 46
13:8 76
13:8–10 76
13:10 76
14:33–36 94
14:33a 39
14:33b 36, 38, 39, 40, 92
14:33b–38 139
14:34 40, 139
14:34–35 38, 39
14:36 38, 39, 40
14:37–38 39, 40
15:12 77

15:12–16 77, 78
15:13 77
15:14 77
15:15 77
15:16 77
15:17 77
15:19 77

2 Corinthians
9:7 34
11:24 69
13:5 102

Galatians
Book of 114
2:11–14 112n, 113
3:12 120
3:28 92, 110
5:3 110

Ephesians
1:7 35
1:18–20 34
2:1–2 69
2:7 69
5:21–30 141
6:12 135

Philippians
2:6–11 48
2:12 68
2:12–13 114n
3:15b 46
4:10–12 116
4:13 115

Colossians
Book of 114

1 Thessalonians
Book of 114
4:13–18 105

2 Thessalonians
Book of 114

1 Timothy
2:11–15 41, 92, 94, 139
2:13 40
2:15 142
3:11 94
6:20 88n3

2 Timothy
1:15 113
4:10 32

Hebrews
1:4 70
3:1 116
3:6b 84
3:14 84
10:7 135
10:12 69
11 72
11:13 69, 71
11:17 31

James
Book of 114
3:6 58

1 Peter
1:24 69
3:7 93
4:1 77

2 Peter
1:4 103n29

1 John
1:6 35
1:7 34
2:3–5 54
2:22 101
2:24 69
3:6 54, 100
3:9 100
4 107
4:2 101
4:8 117
5:21 69

Jude
Book of 114

Revelation
2–3 113
2:13 36
2:26 82
5:9 35
7 90
20:1–6 141
20:4 69
21:4 115
22:22 91